Scott E. Friedman

FAMILY BUSINESS AND POSITIVE PSYCHOLOGY

New Planning Strategies for the 21st Century

Printed in the United States of America.

17 16 15 14 13 5 4 3 2 1

Library of Congress Cataloging-in-Publication Data

Friedman, Scott E., 1958-
    Family business and positive psychology : new planning strategies for the 21st century / by Scott E. Friedman.—First edition.
        pages cm
    Includes bibliographical references and index.
    ISBN 978-1-62722-169-6 (print : alk. paper)
1. Family-owned business enterprises—Law and legislation—United States. I. Title.
    KF1466.F75 2013
    346.73'0668—dc23

                                                                                    2013020177

Other Books by
Scott E. Friedman

Secrets from the Delphi Cafe: Unlocking the Code to Happiness (with Bob Rich)
The Successful Family Business
How to Profit by Forming Your Own Limited Liability Company
How to Run a Family Business (with Michael Friedman)
The Law of Parent-Child Relationships
Sex Law: A Legal Sourcebook on Critical Sexual Issues

Dedication

This book is dedicated to my family, who, once again, supported me while I worked long and difficult hours to complete this book. I hope that the effort will benefit other families.

"Although a feeling of awe at the capability of humans is clearly justified, there is a large difference between a deep sense of admiration and the assumption that our reasoning abilities are perfect."

Dan Ariely, *Predictably Irrational*, at page xix

"By and large...the idea that our minds are susceptible to systematic errors is now generally accepted."

Daniel Kahneman, *Thinking, Fast and Slow,* at page 10

Contents

Acknowledgments

My gratitude to friends, family, and business partners for their amazing support as I worked to complete this book is expressed here in words only imperfectly.

I would like to thank my colleagues at Lippes Mathias Wexler Friedman LLP for their support and encouragement. I am proud to be a partner at a great law firm where I have the opportunity to work every day with smart, principled, entrepreneurial—and collegial—professionals. In many respects, this book is about the benefits that accrue from working in a positive environment, I can attest to the personal and business advantages that result from having the opportunity to work every day with talented colleagues who are also my friends. Special thanks to our firm's operations manager and my longtime assistant, Judy Clark, who (once again) expertly and patiently helped me prepare this manuscript, in the process often working on countless revisions during the evenings and weekends without being asked.

Special thanks to my daughter, Eliza Friedman, and her University at Buffalo Law School classmate, Chris Larrabee, whose impressive intellect and judgment in editing my manuscript made this a much-improved book. I'd also like to thank Anne O'Neil-White for her valuable assistance in researching certain aspects of the challenges we face in communicating effectively.

Thanks to everyone at the American Bar Association for their work on this project, particularly to Richard G. Paszkiet, director of ABA Entity Book Content Publishing, for his encouragement, guidance, and expert suggestions at every step along the way. The professionals at the ABA make the publishing process rewarding and enjoyable.

I'd also like to acknowledge Dr. Dan Baker, one of our country's preeminent family business consultants and author of best-selling books such as *What Happy People Know* and *What Happy Companies Know*. Dan, who has been on the vanguard of applying the insights from positive psychology in his work with his clients, is a great friend, mentor, and colleague from whom I continue to learn.

Thank you to each of the family businesses and their members with whom I have worked over the years. In many respects, my journey is our journey and I will forever value your trust and confidence in me.

Last but by no means least, I'd like to thank my family for their support and encouragement along the way. My parents, Iris and Irwin Friedman, my parents-in-law, Sylvia and Irwin Pastor, my wife, Lisa, along with my children, Samantha, Andrew, Eliza, Julia, and Madeline, as well as my grandchildren, Owen, Eli, Oliver, and Ethan, all of whom constantly remind me that nothing is more important than family. In particular, my wife, Lisa, not only encouraged me as I worked long days, evenings, and weekends but also offered countless insights and suggestions that have made their way into these pages. Once again, in many respects this is Lisa's book as much as mine.

Preface

Several years after finishing law school in 1983, I married my wife, Lisa, and became what is commonly referred to as a "stakeholder" in her family's beverage business.[1] One year later, we moved from Philadelphia, where I had started my law practice with Montgomery McCracken Walker and Rhodes, to our hometown of Buffalo, New York. Our return to Buffalo provided the opportunity to reconnect with old friends and make new friends, many of whom were stakeholders in their family businesses. Surrounded by—and working increasingly with—families in business, I began to pay closer attention to how the legal profession served this constituency.

The more I worked with and studied family businesses, the more I realized that family businesses are a unique type of enterprise with characteristics often inadequately understood by the lawyers and other professionals who serve them or by the families privileged to be part of them. I don't make that observation "critically," but simply in reference to the high rate at which family businesses fail to transition from generation to generation. For example, many authorities in the field continue to report that seven out of ten family businesses fail to transition from the founder generation to the second generation, and nine out of ten family businesses fail to make it to the third generation.[2]

Wanting to be of greater assistance to my clients, I started reading as much as I could on the subject. I began with books and articles written by and for corporate lawyers. However, most of those resources generally focused on "close corporations" (I can't specifically recall finding a law book that even used the term "family business") and addressed the subjects covered in a law school course on corporations, such as choice of entity, capital structure, and options for managing dissension and deadlock. Recognizing the obvious importance of trust and estate law to family businesses, I turned my attention to such subjects as wills and trusts, buy-sell agreements, and retirement planning.

I became convinced that, while these traditional "legalistic approaches" offer essential planning tools, they are insufficient on their own for the challenging requirements at hand. Family businesses need advisers who can provide counsel on their inevitably complex dynamics, particularly with respect to creating a culture that allows family members, each of whom have unique personalities, needs, and interests, to (1) flourish as individuals, (2) collaborate constructively as partners, and (3) run a business effectively and prosperously. That kind of culture allows for financial returns to nonactive family members while fairly rewarding family members active in the business, and simultaneously encouraging family members to follow their dreams, regardless of whether those dreams are within or outside the family business. Families that successfully create such a culture enhance the likelihood of their businesses flourishing, from generation to generation.

My studies ultimately took me beyond the law and into the fields of management and leadership and, over time, psychology and neuroscience. I increasingly realized that the research, ideas, and information that continue to develop outside the fields of traditional corporate law and trust and estate law are critical to a family's search for individual and collective happiness among its members, as well as to the financial and operational success of the family business.

This continuing learning curve may be evident from my earlier books on family business. In *How to Run a Family Business* (1994, written with my brother Mike Friedman, a partner in Pepper Hamilton's corporate practice group), we considered how traditional corporate planning techniques could be used to help family businesses. In *How to Profit by Forming Your Own Limited Liability Company* (1996), I considered how LLCs, like family limited partnerships, could be used to help address the often complex retirement and estate planning needs of family business owners. The widening scope of my studies and experience is reflected in *The Successful Family Business* (1998), which principally sought to share insights and lessons from the allied professions (e.g., psychology, management consulting, therapy, etc.) that can bring great value to family businesses through such tools as family councils, family constitutions, and statements of core values. Most recently, in *Secrets from the Delphi Cafe: Unlocking the Code to Happiness* (2006, which I coauthored with Bob Rich, chairman of Rich Products, one of the largest family-owned businesses in the world), we wrote a story about a fictional character who learns valuable lessons on how to live a "good life" by drawing on insights from philosophy and positive psychology, as well as from our own experiences. While not in any way styled as a "family business text," *Secrets* has great relevance to family businesses since too many individuals wind up working in their family businesses because it is expected, it is easy, or it is lucrative to do so—rather than because it allows them to pursue their genuine passions and interests.

Following the publication of *Secrets*, I sharpened my focus on the fields of neuroscience, evolutionary biology, and psychology, particularly the developing field of positive psychology. The more I learned about the exciting new findings being generated by researchers in these and related fields, the more I realized that family businesses could benefit from a new book that more explicitly discusses the hidden risks they are exposed to when families decide to work together—as well as the benefits to be garnered by understanding these insights and taking easily applied, yet powerfully effective, countermeasures to protect their personal and business interests. Unable to find such a book after surveying the literature, I approached the American Bar Association and conceptually proposed the book you are about to read.

Since, in many respects, this book is about our "fears" and how to overcome them so that we can flourish and thrive as individuals and organizations, it seems appropriate that I share two of my fears regarding what you are about to read. First, the body of scientific knowledge that informs our understanding of how and why we think and act as we do (sometimes rationally but sometimes not) continues to accumulate. Countless books, articles, and other scholarly material containing information of great benefit to family members and their businesses are widely available. Since I am unaware of any other book that seeks to bridge this body of knowledge, particularly the insights from the science of evolutionary biology and positive psychology, to family businesses, I am excited to share this book with you. The inevitable constraints of space and time, however, preclude a more exhaustive treatment of the existing body of knowledge in this text. While I admit to being tempted by my nature to fret about what I have been forced to "leave out," I will, instead, choose to be satisfied with what I have been able to "put in." As I do so, my sincere hope is that this book will not only prove to be of great benefit to my readers but will also help prompt further work that continues to advance our theoretical and practical understanding of how the science of positive psychology and related disciplines can be used to help more family businesses.

Second, I recognize that some readers may be reluctant to take certain suggestions seriously, perhaps dismissing them as "soft" or "hokey," and they may choose instead to stick with traditional planning tools, techniques, and strategies that they learned in school or through experience and have used ever since. Appreciating the skepticism some readers might have, I have included numerous references to scientific and empirical data that support what I believe to be a new paradigm for working with family businesses, a paradigm that is intended to complement traditional planning tools and strategies, not replace them. For the moment, allow me to briefly note that the ideas and suggestions discussed in this book are informed (and no doubt inspired) by many scholarly journals and highly regarded best-selling books, including *Blink* by Malcolm Gladwell, *Predictably Irrational* by Dan Ariely, and *Thinking, Fast and Slow* by Daniel Kahneman. I'd also like to note that, while starting to write this book at the end of 2011, I found myself at JFK Airport in New York City, returning home following a lecture I had delivered at Columbia University's Family Business Management Program. Having some extra time before boarding the plane, I scanned the titles of new magazines for sale at the airport bookstore. What caught my attention was a magazine with a big iconic yellow smiley face on the cover, emblazoned with the title "The Value of Happiness" in the middle of the smile. The magazine was *Harvard Business Review*'s January–February 2012 issue. It was encouraging to note the increasingly clear recognition of the nexus between "happiness" and "success" by many of the world's most respected authorities on business as well as by many dynamic business executives who continue to oversee thriving companies and organizations. This increased attention to the type of fascinating, relevant, and easily applied scientific insights of the kind you are about to read will prove to be of great benefit to many family businesses that, for the most part, have struggled to survive from generation to generation.

In order to make this book as useful as possible, I have included exercises and activities that you can use to help translate the ideas and suggestions that follow into practice. While this book is not intended to make a reader an expert in all the tools, techniques, and strategies suggested, it should help families and their advisers better appreciate how those who do have such expertise can contribute as part of a team effort to help family members in business together.

There is a great opportunity to build on this book's general theory that family businesses can enhance their likelihood of success through science. I am confident that ongoing work by inspired and creative scientists and professional service providers will suggest new and improved ideas and strategies that will further complement the suggestions and strategies offered in the pages that follow. As a result of the integration of science, business, and law, I am optimistic that more family businesses can—and will—flourish and prosper in the 21st century.

The Tragic Normalcy of Family Business Conflict

1

"We can't solve problems by using the same kind of thinking we used when we created them."

Albert Einstein

Background

While I intend to finish this book on a positive note, I sadly can't start it that way. The statistical data points referenced in this book's Preface reflect the reality that family businesses can be very challenging enterprises. A well-known aphorism used to describe the likelihood of family business failure is "shirtsleeves to shirtsleeves in three generations." Describing the tragic frequency of family business failure in a 2012 issue of *Harvard Business Review*, George Stalk and Henry Foley write:

> Some 70% of family owned businesses fail or are sold before the second generation gets a chance to take over. Just 10% remain active, privately held companies for the third generation to lead. In contrast to publicly owned firms, in which the average CEO tenure is six Years, many family businesses have the same leaders for 20 or 25 years, and these extended tenures can increase the difficulty of coping with shifts in technology, business models, and consumer behavior.[1]

The enormity of the impact resulting from so many family businesses failing to transition from generation to generation is impossible to measure and hard to comprehend. While a reliable database of family business demographics does not yet exist, common estimates suggest that upwards of 90 percent of all businesses in the United States are family owned or controlled.[2] While many of these businesses are small sole proprietorships and closely held corporations, many others are counted among the largest companies in the world. Indeed, 40 percent of the largest Fortune 500 companies are estimated to be family owned or controlled.[3] Family Enterprise USA, a nonprofit 501(c)(3) organization, reports that:

- the United States has approximately 5.5 million family-owned businesses, which generate 57 percent of the nation's GDP;
- family enterprises employ 63 percent of the U.S. workforce;
- 75 percent of all new jobs are generated by family businesses;
- 60 percent of all publicly held U.S. companies are family controlled;
- 95 percent of family businesses engage in some form of philanthropy.[4]

By any standard, family-owned businesses have a huge impact on life in the United States.

> There is no generally accepted definition of a "family business," in part because of the multiple factors that might be considered in seeking to identify a business that might not be wholly owned by a family but, nevertheless, might be "family oriented" and/or controlled. One of the most widely used tools to help professionals assess the degree of a family's influence on a business is the F-PEC scale, which considers three criteria: (1) power (how much influence a family exerts through ownership, governance, and management), (2) experience (which relates to the number of family members in a business and to succession), and (3) culture (which relates the degree to which a family's values are embedded in a business). Developed by Professors Sabine Klein, Joseph Astrachan, and Kosmas Smyrnios, the F-PEC scale has gained theoretical and practical support from academicians and family business authorities and "provides a means to explore all businesses along a continuum from intensive family involvement to no family at all and can be used to help raise awareness of family dynamics and influence in a business."[5]

For a variety of reasons, statistics on the reasons family businesses fail to transition from generation to generation are also impossible to come by. Many businesses are sold because families have attractive financial opportunities to generate capital liquidity and other benefits that exceed the economic returns they might otherwise expect from maintaining their ownership. Others might choose to sell or wind down operations due to the absence of an interested or qualified successor to run the business. Family businesses also struggle with many of the same issues facing non-family businesses, such as competition, access to capital, and adversity caused by a variety of other factors, such as changes in government regulations and destructive weather conditions.

While any failure is unfortunate, family business failure that is caused by family conflict is particularly lamentable, often tragic. Sometimes, such conflict becomes public and might even be the subject of wide press coverage. For example, in February 2012, the BBC News reported that Lee Kun-Hee, the chairman of Samsung, had been sued by his brother over an inheritance from their father. The chairman's brother, 80-year-old Lee Maeng-Hee, filed suit for 700 billion Korean won (about U.S. $623 million), claiming his 70-year-old brother misappropriated certain assets.[6] More frequently, however, the family dissension remains private and confidential. I'm quite confident that most professionals who work with family businesses are sadly all too familiar with family business failures caused by family conflict but, for privacy reasons, publicly reported the sales to be motivated by financial opportunity or supplied other reasons that were merely pretexts. Accordingly, one can only speculate on the number of family businesses that fail to transition as a result of family conflict. Anecdotal experience and the many published accounts of family feuds suggest, however, that failures resulting from family conflict are discouragingly far too common.

> Anyone who would like to read more about how infighting has threatened some of the biggest and best-known family-run companies in the world—including Ford, Gucci, McCain, Guinness, Gallo, and Redstone—should consider *Family Wars: Classic Conflicts in Family Business and How to Deal with Them*, a fascinating book written by Nigel Nicholson, a professor of organizational behavior and psychology at the London Business School, and Grant Gordon, director general of the United Kingdom's Institute for Family Business.

The regularity of failure caused by family conflict might seem incomprehensible to many. After all, our most natural instincts include counting on our parents, children, and siblings to look out for our best interests. Beyond our natural instincts, we are taught to care for our family. Indeed, perhaps one of the best-known biblical verses encourages us to "Honor your father and your mother, that your days may be long in the land that the Lord your God is giving you."[7]

However, the Bible also teaches us that family feuds are as old as Cain and Abel, the two sons of Adam and Eve who grew up outside the Garden of Eden, where Cain worked the fields while Abel tended to the sheep. When God favored Abel's sheep offering over Cain's offering, an enraged Cain killed his brother, thus introducing family strife (and murder) to the world.[8]

The history of the world has been replete with countless instances of intra-family dysfunction and feuding ever since. One of the strangest and most interesting family feuds I am aware of involved two brothers, Adolf and Rudolf

Dassler, who started a shoe company together in their mother's laundry room in Germany, sometime in the 1920s. As their business prospered, sibling tension increased. Sometime during World War II, the brothers' relationship reached a breaking point, apparently the result of miscommunication. Nick Carbone, a journalist writing for *Time* magazine, reports that "[a]fter an Allied bomb attack, Adolf and his wife took cover in a bomb shelter already occupied by Rudolf and his family. 'The dirty bastards are back again,' Adolf said, apparently referring to the planes, but Rudolf thought the comment was an attack against his family."[9] By the end of the war, the brothers' relationship had been irreparably breached and they decided to split their shoe company into two. Carbone notes that "Adolf, who preferred to be called Adi, named his business Adidas, combining his first and last names; Rudolf tried the same with his firm called Ruda, though he later changed it to Puma."[10] The brothers, who built their competing factories on the opposite banks of their hometown's river, apparently never spoke again.

The Inadequacy of Traditional Planning Tools

The traditional tools used by lawyers, accountants, and financial advisers, such as trusts that are often funded by life insurance or ownership agreements with customary provisions that might create voting and nonvoting interests or "buy-sell" rights, seem to have discouragingly little success in reducing family conflict, which seems as prevalent today as it has been at any time in history. Even great financial success offers no immunity to the ravages of family conflict, as we learn from disputes involving some of the wealthiest family business owners in the world that have been widely covered by the press.

Consider the $6 billion lawsuit brought in 2002 by then 19-year-old Liesel Pritzker, a member of one of America's wealthiest families, best known for owning the Hyatt hotel chain, accusing her father, Robert, and 11 older cousins of looting her trust funds and those of her brother, Matthew.[11] That case finally settled in 2005 with the Pritzker family interests being split between the 11 cousins over a period of time.[12] Liesel and her brother reportedly each received in excess of $450 million as part of the settlement.

In 2011, the Canadian press reported on the trials and tribulations of the Latners, a Toronto-based family whose interests included air cargo, health care, retirement communities, real estate, medical laboratories, and a casino.[13] Albert Latner's many business successes include taking public his home health care company, Dynacare, in the late 1990s and then selling it in 2002 to LabCorp for $480 million. The Latners, along with a consortium led by the Hyatt Group, built the Fallsview Casino Resort in Niagara Falls, Ontario, an investment that has been valued at $1 billion. In spite of Albert Latner's four children each reportedly receiving at least $150 million over the years, they became locked in intra-family disputes and litigation. One newspaper describes this family's struggles in the following report:

> Many friends and family close to the warring siblings maintain that the disputes have nothing to do with money or material goods. The amounts in question, after all, are paltry given the net worth of the individuals involved. Here's how one old friend of the Latner family summed up the situation: *"The real story revolves around the characters themselves, their petty jealousies, deep-rooted anger over insults, both real and perceived, long simmering grudges and a father who, despite the success he achieved in the business world, proved unwilling or incapable of exercising his influence to moderate these inappropriate behaviors."* The friend added that he doesn't see anyone backing down any time soon.[14]

How is it that so many families who start their business journeys together filled with love and trust in each other—as well as optimism for their business enterprises—so often wind up in conflict, including as adversaries in the courtroom? Clearly the family tragedies experienced by wealthy families such as the Pritzkers, Latners, and Lees suggest that the root cause of family conflict is much more complicated than business struggles, financial challenges, or the inability to access high-quality professional advisers. What insidious factors then are at work inside a family business that are capable of poisoning relationships genetically hardwired to be loving and supportive to a point where there is so much mistrust and animosity that conflict and consequent business failure seem, at times, almost inevitable?

An Introduction to Seven Key Failure Factors

Family businesses are extremely complicated enterprises characterized by the interdependent relationships between (1) individual family members, (2) members of management, (3) employees, and, in some instances, (4) nonfamily investors/owners. Within these various systems and subsystems are stakeholders with different values, attitudes, and perspectives. For example, perhaps one family member, inactive in the business but dependent on annual dividends, might be more risk averse than another family member who, working in the business, might be more entrepreneurial and inclined to take a chance in order to capture what he or she perceives as an exciting new opportunity. Indeed, because of the overlapping nature of these relationships, one or more individuals within any particular family business might occupy multiple roles (such as those of a parent, child, cousin, and employee). This overlap could potentially create some internal personal dissonance about whether a decision is "good" or "bad" based on whether, for example, the individual is considering a major decision (such as whether to fire a son or daughter who is underperforming) as a family member or as a member of the management team.

Figure 1 shows some of the traditional differences between "family values" and "business values."

Figure 1: Differing Value Systems

Family Values	Business Values
Emotionally based	Data/information based
Inherited/Lifetime membership	Earned membership of defined duration
Equality	Equitability
Supportive/forging	Mistakes have consequences
Closed group	Open group

Beyond the inherent complexity of a family business resulting from these obviously overlapping systems, science—principally neuroscience, evolutionary biology, and evolutionary psychology—offers great insights that can help us appreciate how (and why) our minds sometimes work imperfectly—at least for the tasks at hand—in ways that manifest themselves in behaviors that too frequently culminate in the impairment or destruction of family relationships and the failure of their businesses. For example, as we will learn later, our minds can easily fool us into believing that: (1) we are paying attention, when we aren't; (2) we recall facts accurately, when we don't; and (3) we process information rationally on the basis of facts and data, when actually we are being driven by our underlying emotions, biases, and prejudices.

The intersections occurring in a business made up of stakeholders with uniquely personal values, styles, priorities, emotions, passions, and interests would be complex and challenging to manage in a world constituted exclusively by "rational" men and women. Unfortunately, while notions of rationality might have their place in economic textbooks, the real world constantly reminds us that people are people: often irrational, inexperienced, and/or naïve. We all are prone to making suboptimal decisions and taking correspondingly ill-advised action. The negative manifestations of these suboptimal choices can result in family arguments on subjects that range from the pettiest of issues to the most significant. Any family business is susceptible to experiencing these negative manifestations, the consequences of which include lost intra-family trust that, in turn, impairs a family's ability to act cohesively and effectively over time, and, ultimately, often results in tragic family conflict and business failure.

Gary Marcus, a professor of psychology at NYU, writes that:

> [W]e routinely take whatever memories are most recent or most easily remembered to be much more important than any other data . . . Some of the world's most mundane but

common interpersonal friction flows directly from the same failure to reflect on how well our samples represent reality . . . Studies show that in virtually any collaborative enterprise, from taking care of a household to writing academic papers with colleagues, the sum of each individual's perceived contribution exceeds the total amount of work done. We cannot remember what other people did as well as we recall what we did ourselves—which leaves everybody (even shirkers!) feeling that others have taken advantage of them. Realizing the limits of our own data sampling might make us all a lot more generous.[15]

These multidimensional, interpersonal intersections in a family business are commonly manifested or revealed by or through the Seven Failure Factors:

1. Negative culture.
2. The subordination of individual "fit" to "convenience" in employment decisions.
3. Counterproductive communication patterns and styles.
4. Unprincipled decision making.
5. Insular perspectives.
6. Limited repertoire of techniques to prevent and manage conflict.
7. Technically designed plans that ignore family dynamics.

These failure factors work (often silently and imperceptibly at first) to corrode the fabric of family trust that helped create the business in the first place. Because these factors all stem from our great but nevertheless flawed brains, any family business with one failure factor is likely to have other failure factors, the aggregate effect of which is to increase the likelihood of serious jeopardy to family relationships over time, logically explaining why nine out of every ten family businesses fail to transition from the first generation to the third generation.

In *Family Wars: Classic Conflicts in Family Business and How to Deal with Them*, family business authorities Grant Gordon and Nigel Nicholson write:

People often think that the most pernicious source of conflict is "personality." Personality certainly is a key element, but it is more a condition than a cause. It often adds more colour than heat to a dispute . . . *But the real killer is trust—or lack of it. Extreme incompatibilities of personality can make it more difficult to get on the same wavelength, but we don't always mistrust people we know we are different from in character. Lack of trust comes from whatever leads one person to see another as unreliable, inconsistent, devious or duplicitous.*[16]

Mapping Trust

My work over the years suggests that families in business together generally start working with a high level of trust in each other that allows them to work effectively as teammates. Because these failure factors are not typically identified as a threat to family business sustainability, they are neither managed nor controlled. As a consequence, each of the failure factors chips away at the bonds of trust, until eventually trust is so diminished that family members are unable to work together.

Figure 2 illustrates how these failure factors erode trust among family members, ultimately making it extremely difficult for them to continue working together. Family trust might diminish so much that, as it touches the horizontal axis, family members are consumed by fighting each other, whether in or outside the courtroom. This theory of failure is not, however, dependent on families actually hitting that level of conflict. It might be the case that trust is simply so diminished that families are unable to make necessary decisions in a constructive manner. At a certain point unique to every family, it no longer makes sense for the family to remain in business together.

Figure 2

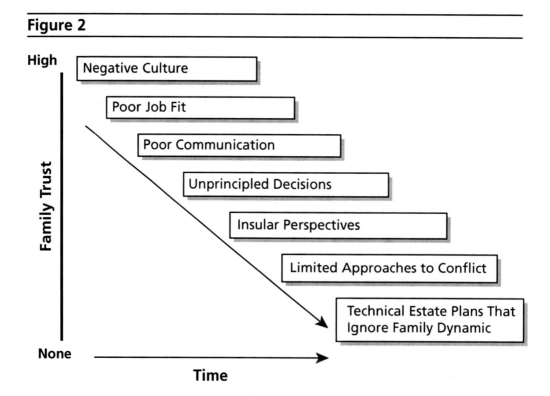

To appreciate how these Seven Failure Factors work, I have found it helpful to start by considering that business activity is a function of the countless decisions made every day, decisions that drive action, which, in turn, determines short-term success or failure and whether a business flourishes or fails in the long run. These decisions can range from the most important choices that need to be made, such as whether to pursue (or stay in) a business sector, or what marketing strategy should be adopted, to "trivial" decisions, such as who gets a parking space—and which one—in the company parking lot. If these decisions are not intelligently and fairly made, intra-family trust and confidence will erode and families will have little chance of sustaining their enterprise.

Many great books have been written about the importance of trust. One of my favorites is Stephen M.R. Covey's best-selling book, *The Speed of Trust*, which he begins by observing that:

> There is one thing that is common to every individual, relationship, team, family, organization, nation, economy and civilization throughout the world—one thing which, if removed, will destroy the most powerful government, the most successful business, the most thriving economy, the most influential leadership, the greatest friendship, the strongest character, the deepest love.

> On the other hand, if developed and leveraged, that one thing has the potential to create unparalleled success and prosperity in every dimension of life. Yet, it is the least understood, most neglected, and most underestimated possibility of our time. That one thing is trust.[17]

Too many family businesses have taken trust for granted and, insensitive to how quickly it can be lost, have paid the high price of family conflict and business failure as a result.

New Strategies for Family Businesses (Seven Success Factors)

Whether to promote continuing family harmony on a prophylactic basis or to counteract the toxic effect of the Seven Failure Factors on family relationships,

I believe families in business together must take steps to intentionally and purposefully design and implement organizational strategies and plans along with accompanying complementary governance structures to reinforce trust among family members and to bring out the best in each individual. Strategies, structures, and safeguards can give every family member and stakeholder a sense that decisions made in their business are fair, principled, and smart. When familial trust has been organizationally and structurally established, other "traditional" planning strategies, such as estate plans, retirement plans, and succession plans, can be executed more smoothly and effectively; until then, however, traditional planning in a "low trust" environment is likely to result in procrastination and disappointment.

Historically, too many family businesses have lacked that extraordinary family leader and wise counsel who can lead them safely through the minefields created by the Seven Failure Factors to create sustainable organizations and strong families. Fortunately, every family business can easily and reliably deploy certain proactive mechanisms and safeguards—which I refer to as the Seven Success Factors because of their great promise to increase the statistics of family businesses successfully transitioning from generation to generation. These success factors are:

1. Create a positive culture.
2. Promote job "fit" over "convenience."
3. Improve communication challenges through humility.
4. Clarify and commit to core principles.
5. Establish professional governance structures.
6. Find constructive ways to resolve disagreements to preempt conflict.
7. Complement traditional planning strategies with insights from positive psychology.

Several of these success factors (such as having boards of directors and dispute resolution mechanisms) are well known to business lawyers, although their particular relevance and application in the family business context might be unfamiliar to some. Other success factors (such as mission and vision statements, family councils, family constitutions, and ground rules for effective meetings) may be less familiar to some attorneys but are commonly used by other experienced professionals who regularly work with family businesses, including psychologists and consultants. Yet other success factors, particularly those informed by the science of positive psychology, have received increased attention in business schools, publications, and in many leading businesses, but have not yet been widely used as part of family business planning.

I believe that all of these factors are essential to the success of a family business and reflect an interesting consistency between the ageless wisdom of great philosophies, religion, and modern science. Although the contributions of religion and philosophy (including as applied to business) are well known,[18] I am unaware of any other book that has sought to apply the insights gleaned from the empirical data derived through scientific studies to family businesses. These insights not only inform our understanding of why and how the Seven Failure Factors can naturally and easily occur in any family business but also suggest why the Seven Success Factors can serve as powerful new strategies and tools that can complement more traditional planning strategies and tools.[19]

Let's continue by turning to a brief introduction of the science of positive psychology as we begin to appreciate how it can be applied by every family that wants to enhance its opportunities for business success while preserving family harmony, perhaps most importantly by creating a positive and nurturing culture.

Chris DeRose, a principal in NTC Marketing, a successful family business headquartered in Buffalo, New York, that imports millions of cans of fruit each year as the exclusive North American licensee of Libby's, recognizes the importance of "trust" in his family's business, which today is run by Chris, his two brothers, Mike Jr. and Dave, and their father, Mike DeRose Sr.

Observing that his family has benefited by applying the same trust-building principles it applies when building and fostering its manufacturing and retail partnerships, Chris notes that "members of his family strive to have the same level of respect for each other that they share with their manufacturing or retail partners." Chris credits his family's focus on trust as the foundation for a productive working environment in their family business, where family members are genuinely interested in each other's welfare and no one would act without considering how contemplated actions might affect other family members.

Quotations

"Family quarrels are bitter things. They don't go by any rules. They're not like aches or wounds; they're more like splits in the skin that won't heal because there's not enough material."

F. Scott Fitzgerald

"The moment there is suspicion about a person's motives, everything else he does becomes tainted."

Mahatma Gandhi

"I don't believe an accident at birth makes people, sisters or brothers. It makes them siblings, gives them mutuality of parentage. Sisterhood and brotherhood is a condition people have to work at."

Maya Angelou

The Promise of Applied Positive Psychology | 2

"If civilization is to survive, we must cultivate the science of human relationships—the ability of all peoples, of all kinds, to live together, in the same world at peace."

Franklin D. Roosevelt

Background: Failure Factor 1 (Negative Culture)

After years of working with and studying family businesses, I am convinced that the existence of a negative culture is the single most important factor behind the failure of many family businesses. It is therefore appropriately Failure Factor 1 (each of the other six failure factors will be discussed in subsequent chapters). Ironically, many business executives and professional advisers have historically been more concerned with the so-called hard factors—quantifiable business metrics like profits, losses, assets, and liabilities—while tending to largely ignore the importance of qualitative factors that contribute to a positive work environment and the related well-being of the individuals who work there. Recent and ongoing discoveries in the field of positive psychology and neuroscience have established with empirical data that creating a collegial and supportive work environment improves not only organizational quality of life but the likelihood of enhancing the bottom line and driving business success as well. Accordingly, the "soft factors" not only matter, they matter more than anything.

Shawn Achor, a leading authority on positive psychology and a prominent business consultant, begins one of my favorite books, *The Happiness Advantage*, by acknowledging the commonly held belief that hard work creates success, in turn creating the ability to enjoy life and find happiness.[1] Unfortunately, the facts suggest that this belief is backward. Supporting his conclusion, Achor writes that "more than a decade of groundbreaking research in the fields of positive psychology and neuroscience has proven in no uncertain terms that the relationship between success and happiness works the other way around. Thanks to this cutting-edge science, we now know that happiness is the precursor to success, not merely the result. *And that happiness and optimism actually fuel performance.*"[2]

Referring to "a study of nearly every scientific happiness study available—over 200 studies on 275,000 people worldwide," Achor notes that "[t]heir findings exactly matched the principles I was teaching [at Harvard]—that happiness leads to success in nearly every domain, including work, health, friendship, sociability, creativity, and energy."[3]

To best understand why creating a positive culture is so critical to family business success, we must first explore some important insights into how evolutionary forces shaped our brains. Over the course of hundreds of thousands of years, our brains evolved in a manner that enhanced our ability to survive in a dangerous world. Today, those same evolutionary adaptations can cause us to think and react in a manner that often sews the seeds for family business failure.

Basic Architecture of the Brain

The human brain, responsible for controlling our memory, vision, hearing, and body movement, is an amazing organ. It is no exaggeration to say that our brains—more than anything else—distinguish us from the rest of the animal kingdom. As prominent scientist Frans de Waal suggested, "Darwin wasn't just provocative in saying that we descended from apes—he didn't go far enough . . . . We are apes in every way, from our long arms and tailless bodies to our habits and temperament."[4] This distinctly human organ allows us to contemplate, to communicate, and to create in uniquely powerful and extraordinary ways. Indeed, the human brain is generally considered the crowning accomplishment of evolution.

While acknowledging this accomplishment, scientists now know that the human brain is the product of one system piled on top of another system—piled on top of yet another system. NYU Professor Gary Marcus characterizes our brain structure as a "kluge"—a term more typically used to describe a clever cobbling together of poorly matched components in order to create a surprisingly workable solution to a problem.[5]

The brain's "kluginess" results from its development of three main structures, commonly described as the hindbrain, midbrain, and forebrain. Each of these has multiple components that are richly interconnected to each other and are generally responsible for increasingly higher-order functionality and responsibilities that are the by-products of evolutionary advances through natural selection.

The oldest part of our brain, the hindbrain or "ancestral brain," is positioned on top of the spinal cord and includes the cerebellum, brain stem, and upper region of the spinal cord. It is responsible for controlling the most basic functions of survival, such as regulating the beating of the heart and breathing. The midbrain (positioned between the hindbrain and forebrain) includes structures that process information, allowing us to see and hear. The forebrain is the forward-most part of the brain, located in front of the midbrain, and it includes the cerebrum, the largest part of the brain. The cerebrum contains two hemispheres, sometimes referred to as "left brain" and "right brain." The forebrain is also the most advanced part of the human brain and it most clearly distinguishes us from other animals, storing memories and controlling higher cognitive functions such as those that allow us to create art, music, and technological inventions.

> Colorfully describing the brain's architecture, Sharon Begley writes that "with modern parts atop old ones, the brain is like an iPod built around an eight-track cassette player."[6]

While our brains allow us to experience life in wonderful ways, we are human, and they don't function with the precision or reliability of computers. The "kluginess" of our brains results in imprecision, unreliability, and imperfection in how we think and act, often creating a variety of challenges for any family business. One particularly important aspect of "kluginess" is our natural yet counter-productive tendency to react emotionally and instinctively to information and events because of our "fight-or-flight" response. This response is driven by the oldest of our brain's circuitry, our ancestral hindbrain.

Fighting, Freezing, and Fleeing

While traditional biologists and psychologists focus on how the mind works, evolutionary biologists and psychologists focus on why the mind works as it does. Drawing on anthropology, zoology, and archaeology, evolutionary biologists and psychologists are principally concerned with how and why the human brain developed in ways that affect how we think and feel today.

In *The Science of Fear*, Daniel Gardner writes that the central insight of evolutionary psychology is that *"our brains were simply not shaped by life in the world as we know it now*, or even the agrarian world that preceded it."[7] The organ that evolved in the savannah is now called upon to make decisions in the city. This observation has enormous implications for anyone striving to live life well, for organizations, and, of particular interest here, for family businesses.

Living in hunter-gatherer societies, the likelihood of survival was enhanced as our ancestral brains evolved to automatically react to danger. This automatic response is a result of various body functions working smoothly and efficiently together, including the nervous system signaling the release of adrenaline and cortisol, hormones that cause the heart to pound faster, muscles to tighten, blood pressure to rise, and senses to become sharper. The flooding of these hormones into our bodies creates, even if only temporarily, increased strength and stamina, sharper reaction time, and sharper focus—preparing the body to face the emergency or danger at hand.

Harvard physiologist Walter Cannon is credited with having discovered this hardwired response, described as "fight or flight." This is a classic example of the success of natural selection. For most of human history, delayed reaction time was often fatal. The ability to act (or react) immediately and think later was functionally enhanced by our ancestral brain offering only three limited reactions when faced with a threat—to fight, to flee, or to freeze. Those of our ancestors who stood still when facing a saber-toothed tiger in order to consider additional options probably didn't last long enough to pass down their genes.

Fighting, freezing, and fleeing are aptly characterized as reactions, not "choices," because of the instinctual and immediate nature of these responses. In *The Ancestral Mind*, Harvard Professor Gregg Jacobs writes that the oldest part of the human brain is responsible for "ensuring basic animal survival by using sensory information to see to it that what takes place inside (our internal physiology) responds to the moment-by-moment requirements of what's outside (our environment, opportunities, and threats). As such, [this part of our brain] is grounded in the here and now; attending to the details that matter immediately."[8]

Even though we have "evolved" as a species through the accumulation of knowledge that has enabled discoveries, inventions, and countless technological innovations, our brains continue to respond instantly when faced with a threatening situation in much the same way it did for our ancestors. These physiological features serve us well in countless important ways today. For example, we might not have time to carefully reflect on the various options available to us when, while driving a car, a young child suddenly dashes into the street. Our brain's hardwiring reacts almost instantly, creating a physical response that prompts us to swerve or slam our foot on the brake and, hopefully, avoid an accident.

The ancestral brain's functionality is also demonstrated through stories of extraordinary strength and agility, conferring what sometimes seems like super-powers to ordinary people. Consider, for example, the following story reported by the press:

> It was Sunday afternoon in Desoto, Texas when Princess Goodwin decided to spend some time with her good friends Pastor Eric Johnson and his family. Suddenly, a car came barreling through the home window crashing into their living room. It was being driven by a drunk driver.
>
> The car hit the couch on which Princess was sitting with 2-month old baby Kendal, her godchild. As soon as she saw the car rushing towards them, Princess held the baby above her head to save her from being hit . . .
>
> "The amazing thing is, Princess had the baby held over like this over the car, so she literally sacrificed herself in order to save the baby," [the friend] said. Baby Kendal only had a scratch on her eye.
>
> Princess [who survived with only injuries to her left leg] later said, "I think the normal instinct would have been to cover, but I raised her," she said. "I think it was nothing but God who lifted her over."[9]

In addition to driving physical responses when we perceive a threat, the ancestral brain is also responsible for the accompanying *emotional* responses we feel in circumstances when we feel threatened. While many of us may be unfamiliar with the biological mechanisms at work in our bodies, we are all quite familiar with how we feel when we are forced to respond to a threat at hand, experiencing emotions that include stress, anxiety, and fear. Consider the above example of having to slam on the car brakes to avoid hitting a child who has run into the street. We might easily imagine the emotional (stressful) feelings resulting from our need to respond to that threat.

The Ancestral Brain and the Perception of Threats

Our ancestors were able to enhance their likelihood of survival by developing brains that allowed them to react almost instantly not only to real threats but to potential threats as well. This ability resulted from processing information sug-gesting pending danger *before* the threats revealed themselves. Because our ancestors often had little or no time to react when encountering dangerous wild prey, anticipating danger was, like reaction speed, an obvious and complemen-tary virtue. In short, our brains evolved so as to not only promote quick reactions but to do so on the basis of fleeting and limited information. Our brains' ability to anticipate threats often serves us well today. For example, we might tend to steer clear of dark alleys or unsavory-looking characters when walking alone at night. Better to be on guard when sensing danger than to wait until danger actually presents itself, or it might be too late.

> Fears of snakes, spiders, and other animals are much more common than fears about electric sockets or driving a car—even though more people are killed by electricity and car accidents. Professor Martin Seligman proposes what he refers to as a "prepared learning" theory to suggest that evolution has bequeathed humans with an innate sensitivity to certain situations that were hazardous to our ancestors. This sensitivity relies on dedicated brain circuits to promote quick and automatic reaction to survival threats that have been passed down through our genes, even though they may no longer be meaningful threats to survival for most people today.

Although our ancestral brain's ability to perceive and anticipate threats can serve us well, this evolutionary adaptation can just as easily cause us to prematurely rush to judgment on the basis of incomplete and imperfect information, or sometimes without any information at all.[10]

Mark Twain once quipped that he was "an old man and [had] known a great many troubles, but most of them never happened." I'm sure we can all think of countless examples where we wrongly perceived the existence of something that concerned or bothered us but that never materialized. This rush to judgment can be responsible for creating many unnecessary problems in family businesses today. I am aware of family feuds that began over trivial circumstances like delays in responses to e-mails that caused people to make unfounded assumptions that they were being ignored, in turn, creating anger-driven reactions.

Ancestral Brain Functioning in Business Today

Our ancestors' behaviors were driven by a variety of life-threatening fears that, of course, are generally no longer relevant in developed countries today since many of the wild beasts that once threatened human survival are now extinct or confronted mostly in the safe haven of a local zoo. However, from an evolutionary timeline perspective that measures the early existence of *Homo sapiens* from approximately 500,000 years ago, this reduction in the level of threat to our survival that has occurred in only the past hundred years or so is insignificant. Dan Gardner eloquently expresses this point when he observes that "[i]f the history of our species were written in proportion to the amount of time we lived at each stage of development, two hundred pages would be devoted to the lives of nomadic hunter-gathers. One page would cover agrarian societies. The world of the last two centuries—the modern world—would get one short paragraph at the end."[11]

Reactions and attendant emotions generated from our ancestral brains continue to serve us well today. As Professor Gregg Jacobs explains, "negative emotions in response to signals from the outside world . . . often keep us alive by keeping us alert and can motivate us to make important life changes."[12] Driven by brains that have evolved over evolutionary time periods, we continue to feel emotions and process information today in certain ways that are the result of our ancestors' need to make decisions and react quickly in order to survive in a dangerous and threatening world. Today, however, once our fight-or-flight response is activated, we typically don't fight or flee in the traditional sense. Instead, when we are faced with our modern-day forms of stress—say an arrogant or rude colleague or customer—our brains continue to process information and events as if they were life-threatening, triggering our hardwired fight-or-flight response. As a result, without the exercise of self control, we are prone to overreacting—which is typically counterproductive and only exacerbates a heated situation.

> The correlation between diminished trust and ancestral brain functioning is now well understood. For example, in discussing the stress experienced by enemies in the workplace, Brian Uzzi and Shannon Dunlap write:
>
>> Many well-intentioned efforts to reverse rivalries fail in large part because of the complex way trust operates in these relationships. Research shows that trust is based on both reason and emotion. If the emotional orientation toward a person is negative—typically because of a perceived threat—then reason will be twisted to align with those negative feelings. This is why feuds can stalemate trust: New facts and arguments, no matter how credible and logical, may be seen as ploys to dupe the other side. This effect is not just psychological; it is physiological. *When we experience negative emotions, blood recedes from the thinking part of the brain, the cerebral cortex, and rushes to its oldest and most involuntary part, the "reptilian" stem, crippling the intake of new information.*
>>
>> *Most executives who decide they want to reverse a rivalry will, quite understandably, turn to reason, presenting incentives for trustworthy collaboration. But in these situations, the "emotional brain" must be managed before adversaries can understand evidence and be persuaded.*[13]

There are a variety of ways in which we might regularly experience stress as a result of our ancestral brain kicking in, such as before having to speak in public (which explains why so many people are reportedly more afraid of public speaking than dying). Within a family business, stakeholders might worry about their children, about their parents, or about how little money they have in the bank. And they are prone to worrying that if someone has more money in the bank than they do, that they aren't doing well enough. Employees might worry about how they are doing, whether they will get the promotion and raise they believe they deserve, or whether they will be asked to find a new job or be forced into early retirement. Business owners might also experience many fears, such as the fear of losing a sale, missing an exciting opportunity, or losing ground to competition.

Family businesses can be particularly fertile breeding grounds for countless such fears. Fears might originate for both business reasons, such as those examples noted above, and for family reasons, such as when a family member fears that another family member is unfairly making more money than he or she is making, receiving greater benefits and perks from the family business, or has greater (yet unwarranted) decision-making authority than he or she does. Family members may also fear that they are not receiving sufficient recognition for their accomplishments and the success of the business (or they may have the reciprocal fear of being blamed for business problems and mistakes). Businesses other than those that are family owned can certainly have destructive negative cultures but such conditions are only the result of poorly managed business fears since there are no family dynamics to manage.

These taxing situations to which our bodies react automatically can negatively affect our emotional and physical health and well-being, particularly if we are ill-equipped to manage the stress. As a result, the fight response is often manifested in angry and argumentative behavior, while the flight response is manifested through social withdrawal, substance abuse, and so on.

In short, beyond the heart attacks, strokes, and related diseases that stress can cause, there are less serious but nevertheless important ramifications to family businesses as a result of our brains' hardwiring continuing to function in the 21st century in much the same way as it did tens of thousands of years ago.

One particularly common fear that family members in business together experience is that other family members are getting higher salaries or benefits than they are. This subject has been widely considered by psychologists in a number of fascinating studies. Consider, for example, the following summary from one study on "keeping up with the Joneses":

Pay level satisfaction has been the focus of much empirical and theoretical work in the last three decades. Much research has focused on the referents that people use in assessing pay level satisfaction . . .

Results in two different samples indicated that upward comparison significantly predicted pay level satisfaction, even when we controlled for lateral and downward comparison as well as other variables. *One possible explanation for this finding is that most people consider themselves above-average performers and therefore expect that an upward comparison is relevant.* A second plausible explanation is that an upward comparison provides useful information for one's assessment of an attribute. More research is needed to identify which of these explanations is correct.[14]

Because most people consider themselves above-average performers, establishing compensation differentials in a family business without compelling justification can create big problems.

These fear-based responses are particularly pernicious because of how easily they can be triggered by perceived threats. Consider the example of a family member who sends an e-mail to someone and, not hearing back immediately, assumes he is being disrespectfully ignored when, in fact, that party is busy on another matter and simply unable to more promptly respond. It also seems quite common for family members to have widely different perceptions about "perks." I have worked with many families over the years where siblings conclude that those working in the business are unfairly rewarded with additional perks, such as tickets to sporting events, all-expense paid trips to conventions at destination locations, and meals at fancy restaurants. At the same time, siblings working in the business often perceive those perks as after-hour obligations that take them away from home and personal time. Our unique perspectives on reality can diverge and create misunderstandings and, if unresolved, conflict can easily result.

It never ceases to amaze me how our propensity to react in "fear mode" can seemingly create problems out of thin air. Conversations might, in the course of a formal meeting or informal gathering over the dinner table, turn to a problem that needs to be solved. The very act of considering the problem and searching for a solution might cause a family member to feel, rightly or wrongly, as if she is being blamed. It is not uncommon for a family member, reacting to the threat of being blamed for a problem and feeling fingers pointed her way, to clam up (a modern-day form of "freezing"), to become defensive and argue disagreeably (a modern-day form of "fighting"), or simply to get up and leave the meeting or dinner table (a modern-day form of "fleeing").

Psychologist and best-selling author Dr. Dan Baker described our modern-day challenges that result from our evolutionary heritage when he writes in *What Happy People Know*:

> The forces of evolution, by their very nature, endowed [our neurological] fear system with tremendous power, because in the brutal early epochs of mankind, it alone kept us alive. It gained us the hair-trigger capacity to spring into action at the first hint of threat. The automatic fear response became faster than the process of rational thought, faster than experiencing the feeling of love, faster than any other human action. And thus we survived. But in doing so, we became hard wired for hard times.
>
> That is our legacy, like it or not.
>
> Unfortunately, in modern life, what is good for survival is often bad for happiness and even for long-term health.[15]

Because our brains are hardwired to process not only actual threats but perceived ones as well, family members can easily misperceive (or misunderstand) events and information and, while in a fear-based mode, experience the same emotions today as our ancestors did when their lives were literally at risk on the grassy tundra. For example, when one sibling feels that his or her parents are favoring another sibling, the reaction in a family business to what is commonly referred to as "sibling rivalry" can be destructive and dramatic, sometimes as a result of explicit behavior and sometimes as a result of "passive aggressive behavior." In my years of experience working with many parents with children in family businesses, I can't recall a single instance where the parents didn't believe they weren't doing everything they could to treat all of their children fairly and equitably. They often find it very difficult to understand how one sibling can believe that the others are being favored.

Fears based on perceived threats can be as dangerous or more so than those that are reality-based. A real threat is usually short lived and resolved one way or another. Our ancestors' fears might have lasted only as long as it took to be eaten or killed. Imaginary fears, however, have a tendency to be more prolonged because the threat never materializes. There is no end to the fear, tension, and other emotions it produces. Unresolved and prolonged fear can easily manifest itself in counterproductive fear-based behaviors that can be problematic for family businesses today.

Common Examples of Fear-Based Behavior Today

As a result of our brains continuing to function in much the same way as the brains of our hunter-gatherer ancestors, we are prone to experience fear and its accompanying negative emotions in many everyday situations that are far from life-and-death matters. Common examples include fears that:

- we will be rejected (such as for a promotion, as a successor, etc.);
- we will be excluded from an exciting business opportunity;
- we aren't being given appropriate responsibility (or we are being given too much responsibility that we won't be able to handle);
- we aren't smart enough;
- our efforts won't be appropriately recognized and credited;
- we will be taken advantage of.

The nature of our fear-based thinking is so pervasive that some billionaires on the Forbes list of the wealthiest people in the world reportedly even worry that they might drop down on the list or (heaven forbid) drop off the list. Our tendency to respond emotionally in this manner too frequently drives inappropriate behavior and gross overreactions, resulting in unnecessary problems. At the extreme, intra-family litigation is really a modern-day form of fighting. Actual fisticuffs, of course, are not unheard of either and I have worked with a number of families over the years that came to me after family members wound up fighting each other.

In many instances, emotions generated as part of our fight-or-flight response can manifest themselves in negative behaviors that are not typically thought of as fear-based, such as:

Greed: the manifestation of our fear that we might wind up with not enough of something we value.

Insecurity: the fear of being perceived as not smart enough, wealthy enough, talented enough, or otherwise good enough.

Arrogance: the adoption of an attitude of superiority to compensate for a fear of being perceived as weak, deficient, or otherwise inadequate.

"Turf-ism": the noncooperation or conflict between those with common goals or interests that results from thinking of colleagues and teammates as competitors.

Lying: the product of a variety of fears, including the fear that telling the truth will result in rejection or create unpleasant consequences.

Cheating: the result of the fear that failing will have adverse consequences, or that a commitment to a relationship will result in lost opportunities.

Anger: the emotional response that prepares us for the fight against a perceived threat or fear.

The attendant consequences of these and related fear-based behaviors in the workplace are clear and stand in stark contrast to those found in a happy environment. Shawn Achor writes that:

> Data abounds showing that happy workers have higher levels of productivity, produce higher sales, perform better in leadership positions, and receive higher performance ratings and higher pay. They also enjoy more job security and are less likely to take sick days, to quit, or to become burned out. Happy CEOs are more likely to lead teams of employees who are both happy and healthy, and who find their work climate conducive to high performance. The list of benefits of happiness in the workplace goes on and on.[16]

The subtle nature of modern-day fears and their typical consequences, such as job stress, fatigue, high absenteeism, and short-term/reactive thinking, can be hard to recognize and address until it is too late. It is no wonder that a family business can be such a perilous endeavor. Fortunately, our fear-based behaviors that create family conflict and a negative work environment can be overridden by another part of our brain that is responsible for creating positive emotions, allowing us to flourish and create a positive, productive workplace culture.

Higher-Order Brain Functioning

The summary overview of evolutionary psychology presented so far remains incomplete. The human brain continued to develop in a variety of ways, ultimately peaking about 500,000 years ago. Most of the more recent growth took place in the part of the brain commonly known as the forebrain or "modern brain" that includes the neocortex. The neocortex, responsible for language, abstraction, and the ability to plan, also gives us the capacity for emotional intelligence, logical thought, creativity, and moral and spiritual sensibilities. Indeed, the neocortex is that part of our brain that makes us distinctly human, allowing us to create technologies with astonishing capabilities, cure diseases, create great art, and accomplish countless other feats.

While our ancestral brain continues to trigger an immediate fight, freeze, or flight response when we feel threatened, our modern brain allows us to pause, catch our breath, and to think logically and intentionally about a situation. This functionality enables us to process facts and information as well as to evaluate options, relationships, and circumstances with insight, intuition, and understanding. Figure 3 highlights several examples of the difference between a fear-based response driven primarily from our ancestral brains and a higher-order response driven primarily from our modern brains.

Figure 3: Differences in Thinking Styles	
Fear-Based Thinking	**Higher-Order Thinking**
Reactive	Strategic
Looks backward to solve problems	Looks forward to possibilities
Assigns blame	Builds cohesion by forgiving
Limited repertoire of ideas	Creative thinking
Angry	Compassionate
Focuses on mistakes	Focuses on lessons
Feels entitled	Feels responsible
Goes through motions (fleeing)	Committed and engaged
Sabotages work	Collaborative
Fears not having enough	Appreciative

Because of our ancestral brain's immediate and preemptive responses to real and perceived threats, we must consciously use our modern brain to override this immediate fear-based response in search of a healthy balance. The decision of families in business together to appreciate the conceptual choices they have and intentionally lead with their higher-order brains can be one of the most important steps they take for their business. In many respects, this recommendation is consistent with the teachings of the world's great religions and philosophies that advocate expressing values such as love, compassion, forgiveness, and integrity—all of which have their origin in the modern brain. For those in business who aren't motivated by philosophy or religion, scientifically derived empirical data is, as described below, now available that also confirms that choosing to focus on positive emotions is not only the key to personal happiness but to the creation of a successful, profitable, and sustainable business as well.

Whole-Brain Thinking

The foregoing suggestion that we should lead with our higher-order thinking to override our fear-based response is not intended to suggest that we should seek to completely ignore our ancestral brain's emotions. The modern, rational brain has its own limitations that must also be understood and managed, as we will explore in later chapters.

The reality is that if we are to live life well, we must find a healthy balance between rational thought and emotion, between our ancestral brain and our modern brain. Professor Gregg Jacobs expresses this point when he writes:

> If we are to improve our lives and see our way toward a more fulfilling future, we must strike a greater balance between thought and emotion, Thinking Mind and Ancestral Mind, as well as establishing an equilibrium between the negative emotions that modern life forces upon us and the positive emotions that are our birthright, and that can help us overcome those negatives . . .
>
>   The choice is not an "either/or." The Ancestral Mind is a resource that balances and mitigates the harmful qualities of the Thinking Mind; it doesn't replace it . . . [17]

In short, we are undoubtedly at our best when we integrate the best aspects of our whole brain, seeking to find a healthy balance that allows us to be logical (intelligent) and sensitive (emotionally intelligent), without being either rigidly logical or hysterically emotional. Good decisions aren't just logical; they are emotional too.

Dan Baker elegantly describes the biology and psychology of the brain, writing:

> The reptilian brain holds instinctual fears and is incapable of higher thought. It cannot process complex emotions such as love. That's why reptiles don't make good pets. A lizard will never learn its name or love its owner.
>
> There's also another storage area for fear, which is located in the second part of the brain to evolve, the mammalian brain . . . Residing in the mammalian brain is the other important culprit in the neurological symphony of fear: the amygdala. The amygdala is a memory center of emotion . . . It's a primitive warehouse for everything that's frightening. . . .
>
> Fortunately, though, the fear system can be overruled by the third major part of the brain, the neocortex. The neocortex was the last part of the brain created during evolution, and it is the last part of the brain that is developed in the womb. . . .

The neocortex evaluates the messages from the two lower areas of the brain, including the constant cries of fear that bubble up from the reptilian brain and the amygdala. It has the amazing ability to say "Nothing is wrong—calm down!"[18]

Baker continues, noting that the feedback we get from our neocortex doesn't always come through and calm us down because fear comes faster, we get overwhelmed, or we get tired. This happens because we are human. Succinctly summarizing the implications of having a brain with three systems, he writes "In every one of us, there is a delicate and shifting balance between the power of the reptilian brain and the power of the neocortex. I call this oscillating balance the dance of the spirit and the reptile. The spirit must lead. That is the key to happiness."[19]

"Everywhere the human soul stands between a hemisphere of light and another of darkness; on the confines of the two everlasting empires, necessity and free will."

Thomas Carlyle

As Daniel Goleman, a noted authority on the subject of emotional intelligence, explains in his best-selling book *Emotional Intelligence*:

The emergency route from eye or ear to thalamus to amygdala is crucial; it saves time in an emergency, when an instantaneous response is required. . . .

In evolutionary terms, the survival value of this direct route would have been great, allowing a quick response option that shaves a few critical milliseconds in reaction time to danger . . . "But it's a quick-and-dirty process; the cells are fast, but not very precise." . . .

. . . But in human emotional life that imprecision can have disastrous consequences for our relationships, since it means, figuratively speaking, we can spring at or away from the wrong thing—or person.[20]

The Science of Successful Family Businesses

The insights gleaned from the developing work in fields like neuroscience and positive psychology have great and heretofore much-neglected relevance to family businesses on three principal levels.

First, these insights help explain why family members and key stakeholders—driven by an overreliance on ancestral brains that tend to process information in fear-mode that offers a limited repertoire of modern-day forms of fighting, fleeing, and freezing—almost naturally wind up in a variety of challenging intra-family dynamics that lead from frustration and disappointment to disagreement and then to conflict. Traditional legal planning strategies have ignored these dynamics other than to provide some form of dispute resolution in a shareholder agreement. Such an approach, essentially the same as if a physician were treating a patient's symptoms but not his disease, might work in the short term but it rarely works over a longer term, hence the high failure rate.

Second, these same insights can be used to help family members and key stakeholders to appreciate and manage both their negative emotions and their behaviors by using well-accepted strategies such as improved communication through family meetings and better listening skills that can help mitigate modern-day forms of fighting, fleeing, and freezing.

Third, the insights from positive psychology and neuroscience can be used not simply to help us more effectively manage problems and disagreements but also to suggest strategies that allow us to lead from our strengths and behave consistently with our best virtues. This allows us to tap into our higher-order thinking and live happier and more fulfilling lives rooted in strong, loving, and supportive family relationships.

The proposal to develop and apply new strategies for family businesses that are grounded in science, and to focus on the creation and cultivation of an environment that allows family members and stakeholders to authentically collaborate and leverage their collective wisdom and expertise, represents a fundamental planning paradigm shift for family businesses. So that this proposal is not misunderstood as based on old and recycled notions of the power of positive thinking or generic self-help advice, it is important to say a few words about the science of positive psychology.

The Science of Positive Psychology

Positive psychology has been described as the scientific study of the "conditions and processes that contribute to the flourishing or optimal functioning of people, groups and institutions."[21] While psychology's focus has traditionally been on how to alleviate our problems, positive psychology's focus is on how to bring out the best in people so that they can live happy and productive lives. Positive psychology is intended to complement, not replace, traditional psychology.

Positive psychologists have had to work hard to disassociate themselves from the clichéd "yellow happy face" and its implicit popular recommendation not to worry and to just "be happy." Martin Seligman, a University of Pennsylvania professor who is generally regarded as the father of positive psychology, commented in his most recent book, *Flourish*, that "[t]he primary problem with that title [of his earlier book, *Authentic Happiness*] is not only that it under-explains what we choose but that the modern ear immediately hears 'happy' to mean buoyant mood, merriment, good cheer and smiling."[22] As a science, positive psychology should not be confused with the anecdotal and personal observations of the kind one might find in many traditional self-help books. Such advice might be good (or bad) but it isn't based on scientifically conducted experiments and studies. As Professor Seligman elsewhere observes, "In this quest for what is best, positive psychology does not rely on wishful thinking, self-deception, or hand waving; instead, it tries to adapt what is best in the scientific method to the unique problems that human behavior presents in all its complexity."[23]

Many of the conclusions drawn from positive psychology are neither new nor surprising and are often consistent with the teachings of the world's great religious figures, such as Jesus, Maimonides, Buddha, and Confucius, as well as great philosophers, such as Plato and Aristotle. As one leading scholar has observed:

> Today's positive psychologists do not claim to have invented notions of happiness and well-being, to have proposed their first theoretical accounts, or even to have ushered in their scientific study. Rather, the contribution of contemporary positive psychology has been to provide an umbrella term for what have been isolated lines of theory and research and to make the self-conscious argument that what makes life worth living deserves its own field of inquiry within psychology, at least until the day when all of psychology embraces the study of what is good along with the study of what is bad.[24]

One way to measure the extent of the paradigm shift created by positive psychology is to compare the number of scholarly publications on traditionally important areas of study to the number of publications on subjective well-being. One early analysis of this shift notes that "research output on depression and anxiety exceeds the research output on subjective well-being and psychological well-being by several orders of magnitude. We are encouraged by the fact that research into subjective well-being has increased by a factor of almost 180 (6 publications by 1978 to 1,070 by September 2003)."[25] A number of particular fields of interest in positive psychology have emerged, including the study of strengths, happiness, flow, and mindfulness.

Many well-respected business leaders and scholars continue to promote important insights gleaned through science. Bill George, a professor of management practice at Harvard Business School, former chairman and CEO of Medtronic, and author of best-selling books, including *True North*, *Finding Your True North*, and *Authentic Leadership*, encourages the practice of "mindful leadership"—the practice of being present in the moment, paying attention to your feelings, and keeping in touch with those feelings no matter how stressful the situation. Encouraging the practice of mindful leadership, Professor George describes the benefits he realizes from meditating 20 minutes twice a day in the following passage from his blog on the *Harvard Business Review* network:

> Meditation has been a godsend for me. As an active leader who has held highly stressful roles since my mid-twenties, I was diagnosed with high blood pressure in my early thirties. When I started meditating, I was able to stay calmer and more focused in my leadership, without losing the "edge" that I believe made me successful. Meditation enabled me to cast off the many trivial worries that once possessed me and gain clarity about what was really important. I gradually became more self-aware and more sensitive to the impact I was having on others. Just as important, my blood pressure returned to normal and stayed there.[26]

In recent years, medical studies have found evidence of meditation's many benefits, including protecting against health problems such as high blood pressure, arthritis, and infertility; reducing stress; improving attention and sensory processing; and physically altering parts of the brain associated with learning and memory, emotional regulation, and perspective-taking, which are critical cognitive skills for leaders attempting to maintain their equilibrium under constant pressure.[27]

The following helpful tips on how to meditate come from Mary Jaksch, an author, psychotherapist, and authorized Zen master:

1. **Posture.** Make sure that your spine is upright with your head up.
2. **Eyes.** Keep your eyes open so as to limit time spent drifting away on thoughts and stories.
3. **Focus.** Pay attention to whatever you place in the center of awareness.
4. **Breath.** Paying attention to the breath is a great way to anchor yourself in the present moment.
5. **Counting your breath.** If you are having difficulties settling, you can try counting the breath, an ancient meditation practice.
6. **Thoughts.** When you notice thoughts, gently let them go by returning your focus to the breath. Don't try to stop thoughts;

this will just make you feel agitated. Imagine that they are unwelcome visitors at your door: acknowledge their presence and politely ask them to leave.

7. **Emotions**. It's difficult to settle into meditation if you are struggling with strong emotions. The way to deal with strong emotions in meditation is to focus on the body feelings that accompany the emotion.

8. **Silence**. Nothing beats simple silence. When we sit in silence we actually get to experience what our mind is doing. Steadiness and calmness come from sitting in silence.

9. **Length**. Start with ten minutes and only sit longer if you feel that that is too short. Don't force yourself to meditate longer if you are not ready to do that. In time you might like to extend your meditation to 25 minutes. That's a length that allows you to settle your mind without causing too much stress on your body. Most importantly, shrug off any "shoulds." Some people enjoy sitting for an hour at a time. Others find that they can't sit longer than ten minutes. Do what feels right for you!

10. **Place**. It's lovely to create a special place to sit. You can even make a shrine or an altar that you can face when you sit in meditation. You might like to place a candle on your altar and objects that have meaning to you.

11. **Enjoyment**. Most of all, it's important to enjoy meditation. You might like to try sitting with a hint of a smile. Be kind to yourself. Start sitting just a little each day. It's helpful to establish a daily habit.[28]

Jill Hamburg Coplan writes in *Bloomberg Businessweek* that:

What makes positive psychology different, its proponents say, is a decade of clinical trials, making sometimes controversial use of brain-scanning technology, that have measured and refined what happiness can do. They've looked at how much an upbeat mood, for example, reduces the time it takes a team of doctors to make a tricky diagnosis. They've found that a social worker will make twice as many visits to clients if he or she feels appreciated.[29]

By helping people use their "advanced brains" to identify and leverage their strengths, talents, and virtues, Seligman and his disciples have assembled a growing body of knowledge, backed by empirical data, on how to fuel individual happiness and personal and collective success. It is time for this body of knowledge to be applied to benefit family businesses, and the suggestions set forth in the rest of this book are intended to help accomplish that objective.

Another difference between traditional psychology and positive psychology is that positive psychologists tend to discourage paying too much attention to past mistakes that we might have made, unless the purpose of such focus is to learn lessons.

Traditional psychology also is known for its practice of having patients discuss what is bothering them and venting their emotions. Studies have shown, however, that venting feelings actually exacerbates or causes problems rather than helping.[30]

Positive psychology does not pretend there isn't suffering in the world. Nor does it pretend there aren't problems. Instead, it is based on the premise that we can choose not to suffer (or choose to suffer less than we do) by changing what we think about and how we spend our time. As long as we have the basics for survival—a roof over our heads, food, and health—we can find ways to live our lives well, whatever our particular circumstances.[31] In doing so, positive psychology can help move people beyond the point where there is not simply the absence of stress and to a point where there is a sense of well-being and optimal functioning.[32] The science of positive psychology is helping individuals to be happier and organizations to flourish. As the next chapter explains, positive psychology can also benefit any family business.

Shawn Achor has taught lawyers how to use positive emotions to be happier and more successful. He writes that:

> lawyers have more than three times the depression rate of the average occupational group and that law students suffer from dangerously elevated levels of mental distress. . . . To attack this thorny reality, I taught the seven principles [that are responsible for happiness and success in the workplace] to focus groups of lawyers and law students across the country. We talked about how using a positive mindset could gain them a competitive edge, how building up their social-support systems could eradicate anxiety, and how they could buffer themselves against the negativity that spread rapidly from one library cubicle to another. Again, the results were immediate and impressive. Even in the midst of heavy workloads and the tyranny of impossible expectations, these hard-driving individuals were able to use the Happiness Advantage to reduce stress and achieve more in their academic and professional lives.[33]

Quotations

"The science of psychology has been far more successful on the negative than on the positive side. It has revealed to us much about man's shortcomings, his illness, his sins, but little about his potentialities, his virtues, his achievable aspirations, or his full psychological height. It is as if psychology has voluntarily restricted itself to only half its rightful jurisdiction, and that, the darker, meaner half."

A. H. Maslow

"Whatever else history may say about me when I'm gone, I hope it will record that I appealed to your best hopes, not your worst fears; to your confidence rather than your doubts. My dream is that you will travel the road ahead with liberty's lamp guiding your steps and opportunity's arm steadying your way."

Ronald Reagan

"The oldest and strongest emotion of mankind is fear, and the oldest and strongest kind of fear is fear of the unknown."

H. P. Lovecraft

"As a rule, what is out of sight disturbs men's minds more seriously than what they see."

Julius Caesar

"The enemy is fear. We think it is hate; but it is fear."

Gandhi

"He who fears he shall suffer, already suffers what he fears."

Montaigne, Essays

"Worry often gives a small thing a big shadow."

Swedish Proverb

"Never bear more than one kind of trouble at a time. Some people bear three—all they have had, all they have now, and all they expect to have."

Edward Everett Haled

"That the birds of worry and care fly over your head, this you cannot change, but that they build nests in your hair, this you can prevent."

Chinese Proverb

"Never be afraid to try something new. Remember, amateurs built the ark, professionals built the Titanic."

Unknown

"Rule number one is, don't sweat the small stuff. Rule number two is, it's all small stuff."

Robert Eliot

"Man is fond of counting his troubles, but he does not count his joys. If he counted them up as he ought to, he would see that every lot has enough happiness provided for it."

Fyodor Dostoevsky

Fostering Positive Interpersonal Relationships 3

"Family life is too intimate to be preserved by the spirit of justice. It can be sustained by a spirit of love which goes beyond justice."

Reinhold Niebuhr

Culture and Business

Alexis de Tocqueville's *Democracy in America*, published in 1835, is widely recognized as an authoritative work on early 19th-century culture in this country. One of De Tocqueville's observations that remains relevant today was the contrast he observed between the traditional European practice of primogeniture (by which the bulk of an estate was transferred to the eldest child), and the common practice in this country to more widely distribute assets among all family members. Regardless of what one might think about the fairness of primogeniture, the practice has been credited with allowing many aristocratic families in Europe to more easily transition their estates from generation to generation. With the demise of primogeniture, siblings were more likely to become partners where the assets in an estate included a business. One result has been that siblings (and their children if fortunate enough) need to figure out how to both live and work together. If siblings and succeeding generations are unable to work together constructively, they will be unable to perpetuate their family business over the generations.

Lacking the clear legal control that the oldest son would have had in a different cultural era, siblings and, depending on the family business, cousins, often driven by the negative emotions created in our ancestral brains, frequently find themselves locked in conflict, litigation, and other modern-day forms of "fighting." Without a culture that overrides naturally occurring fear-based behaviors by promoting constructive working relationships between family members, the prospects of destructive intra-family conflict and litigation can, at times, seem almost inevitable.

While family business owners and their professional advisers traditionally spend much time and energy anticipating such problems and seeking to create dispute resolution mechanisms, their continuously high failure rate suggests that if the cultural core of a family business is rotten as a result of excessive, fear-driven behavior and emotion, such traditional problem-solving efforts are likely to be unsuccessful. I believe this accounts for the fact that even many of the most affluent family-owned businesses continue to experience family dysfunction and conflict, notwithstanding their access to sophisticated professional advisers who work hard to develop customized plans intended to ensure the successful transition of their family businesses.

> The limits of family business planning based on the implicit assumption that man is wholly rational is anticipated by Professor Gary Marcus when he observes:
>
>> If mankind were the product of some intelligent, compassionate designer, our thoughts would be rational, our logic impeccable. Our memory would be robust, our recollection reliable. Our sentences would be crisp, our words precise, our language systematic and regular, not besodden with irregular verbs (sing-sang, ring-rang, yet bring-brought) and other peculiar inconsistencies. As the language maven Richard Lederer has noted, there would be ham in hamburger, egg in eggplant. English speakers would park in parkways and drive on driveways, and not the other way around.[1]

Rather than working to resolve disputes and conflicts after they occur, scientific data suggests that a smarter strategy is to focus on ensuring the existence of a positive culture where family members and company stakeholders devote most of their energy to the pursuit of possibilities and the accomplishment of goals, where disagreements of perspectives and opinions are constructively reconciled, and where counterproductive conflict is minimized if not preempted.

This chapter examines some of the compelling empirical findings that culture matters—and what can be done to create and maintain a positive culture in a family business. It explores how to create a culture where stakeholders are genuinely supportive of each other and differences in opinions aren't considered "problematic disagreements," but simply honest conversations that are part of a process designed to move an initiative forward in the most effective manner possible.

Individuals who are happy because they fit well within an organization are more likely to contribute to the existence of a positive culture than individuals who are unhappy because of a poor fit. Accordingly, chapter 4 explores the correlation between having authentically passionate individuals who are capable of handling the responsibilities they are each tasked with and family business success.

An unfortunate collateral aspect of the failure of traditional planning approaches sometimes includes a family's disappointment (or anger) with their professional advisers, and the family might unfairly conclude that these advisers are more concerned with their fees (which often get bigger as problems get worse) than with fixing the family's conflict. Such negative perceptions are particularly unfortunate as most professionals work very hard to help these clients but heretofore haven't been given enough tools to more successfully preempt family fighting.

Positive Psychology Findings

Scientific research in the field of positive psychology, particularly since 1998 when Martin Seligman gave his presidential address to the American Psychological Association, has grown exponentially. Many of these findings are quite interesting, with some even garnering widespread publicity. For example:

- Optimistic people are less likely to die of heart attacks than pessimistic people.[2]
- Happiness is contagious and people who are surrounded by happy friends and family tend to become happier.[3]
- Women who displayed genuine smiles to a photographer at age 18 went on to have fewer divorces and more marital satisfaction than women who displayed fake smiles.[4]
- People tend to exaggerate the impact of both positive and negative events—and, tending to adapt to both good news and bad news, often wind up at the same happiness "set point" over time.[5]
- How you celebrate good events that happen to your spouse is a better predictor of future love and commitment than how you respond to bad events.[6]

Thankfully, scientific research that can be applied to inform our thinking on happiness and success shows no signs of slowing down. New technologies are even helping to generate new data. For example, Matthew Killingsworth, a doctoral student in psychology at Harvard, has created an application for the iPhone that allowed him to recruit more than 15,000 people in 83 countries to randomly report on their emotional states in real time. Among other things, Killingsworth has found that "people's minds wander nearly half the time, and this appears to lower their mood."[7] He writes:

> Wandering to unpleasant or even neutral topics is associated with sharply lower happiness; straying to positive topics has no effect either way. . . . The amount of mind-wandering varies greatly depending on the activity, from roughly 60% of the time while commuting to 30% when talking to someone or playing a game to 10% during sex. But no matter what people are doing, they are much less happy when their minds are wandering than when their minds are focused.[8]

All of this strongly suggests that to optimize our emotional well-being, we should pay at least as much attention to where our minds are as to what our bodies are doing.

As previously observed, many of the scientific findings that inform our understanding of interpersonal relationships are often supported by the timeless insights of religion and philosophy. Great literature can also provide keen insight into the human condition (and, in doing so, has anticipated science), such as in *Anna Karenina*. Leo Tolstoy famously begins his classic Russian novel with the observation that all happy families resemble one another, but each unhappy family is unhappy in its own way. One can fairly interpret Tolstoy's main message to be that all happy families resemble each other because all of his book's "happy characters" are committed to higher-order relationships, genuinely embodying the great virtues of love, compassion, forgiveness, and understanding in their intra-familial relationships. Those of his characters that are driven more by their fear-based ancestral brain thinking tend to unhappily struggle through life.

While positive psychology is broadly interested in individuals, families, groups, organizations, institutions, and communities, there is a considerable amount of scientific research that is particularly relevant to the challenge of creating a successful business enterprise. In *The Happiness Advantage*, Shawn Achor refers to a sweeping meta-analysis of over 200 academic studies by Sonja Lyubomirsky, Laura King, and Ed Diener that found that happy employees have, on average, 31 percent higher productivity; their sales are 37 percent higher;

their creativity is three times higher.[9] In reporting the connection between a positive culture and organizational success, Achor references numerous empirical findings, including the following:

1. Happiness allows us to work longer, faster, and with fewer sick days.
2. People who express more positive emotions are more effective negotiators than those who are neutral or negative.
3. Happiness increases dopamine and serotonin, which increases neural connections and allows us to be more thoughtful and creative.
4. Project teams with encouraging managers perform better than teams whose managers praised less.
5. How something is said (e.g., cheerful vs. hostile) is just as important as what is said.
6. A leader's positive mood is likely to put employees in a positive mood and facilitate the coordination of teamwork.
7. Optimists set more goals than pessimists and are more likely to stay focused on achieving those goals.[10]

One observer, writing in 2009, noted that since 2004, when Case Western Reserve University began a program in Positive Organizational Development, "hundreds of happiness and business researchers have taken on assignments at companies as various as Toyota Motor (TM), Ann Taylor Stores (ANN), BP's (BP) Castrol Marine, and Standard Charter Bank, as well as the Scottish city of Glasgow and the U.S. Navy."[11]

The ongoing findings from positive psychology suggest exciting opportunities for family businesses to create a positive culture that could, among other things, help to:

- engender trust and loyalty among family members and employees and with customers;
- build strong teams;
- encourage new ideas; and
- attract and retain high-level talent.[12]

The endless possible applications of positive psychology to family businesses are only just beginning to receive attention.[13] These insights not only can help counteract the effects of a negative environment, but they can help build a positive culture that can create the foundation for a successful and sustainable family business. Indeed, there is likely no better opportunity to reverse the miserably high statistical failure rate of family businesses than by starting to apply these insights. For that reason, the intentional creation of a positive culture is Success Factor 1.

Suggestions for Creating a Positive Culture

While creativity may be the only limit to how scientific insights might be applied to help a family business, I believe that all families should seek to incorporate the following basic suggestions into their company's culture: focus on being positive; focus on appreciation; practice altruism; practice civility; be supportive; learn to forgive; and be compassionate. Each of these practices will be discussed in turn next.

Focus on Being Positive

I have seen many family businesses in which criticism, even about petty subjects, is robust while enthusiasm and authentic praise, even for major accomplishments and achievements, is in short supply. Family businesses would benefit from being more complimentary, encouraging, constructive—more positive—which can help build stronger bonds in the workplace and among family members.

One of the leading experts in this area, Barbara L. Fredrickson, a psychology professor at University of North Carolina at Chapel Hill, has concluded that, just as there is a fear-based fight-or-flight response, there is a similar yet opposite response when we feel content. Frederickson's theory is premised on the notion that while the fear-based response helped to keep us from being eaten alive, individuals were able to organize as communities because of other chemicals that trigger what she refers to as the "broaden-and-build" state of mind. The broaden-and-build theory posits that when we experience positive emotions, we are more creative, resilient, and likely to make better social connections. Like an upward spiral, positive emotions in turn generate even more positive emotions.[14]

Frederickson also discusses the benefits of promoting positive emotions such as joy, gratitude, interest, hope, pride, amusement, inspiration, awe, and love. The respective powers of negative or positive emotions are increasingly well understood. As one commentator notes, "[P]eople experiencing positive emotions show patterns of thought that are significantly broadened and diverse, flexible, creative, integrative, open to information, and efficient."[15]

Positivity Ratio

Frederickson's studies have led to the demonstration of the existence of what has come to be referred to as a "positivity ratio": the ratio of positive to negative emotions needed to get the broaden-and-build effect. Research has demonstrated that corporate teams are more likely to flourish if they experience three or more positive emotions for every one negative emotion. Stagnating teams have a lower ratio.[16] Positive teams exhibited a number of helpful qualities, including greater openness to new ideas, greater social connections between team members, and enhanced ability to bounce back after disappointments.[17]

Professor Frederickson and Professor Marcial Losada use the term "positive affect" to describe pleasant emotions (e.g., feeling grateful, feeling upbeat, liking) and "negative affect" to describe unpleasant emotions (e.g., irritability, disdain, disliking). They also define "flourishing" to mean living "within an optimal range of human functioning, one that connotes goodness, generativity, growth and resilience."[18] They contrast the state of flourishing with the state of "languishing," which is the experience of living a "hollow" or "empty" life.

Their research convincingly establishes that affect, whether positive or negative, is statistically correlated with whether people will flourish or languish. Individuals, marriages, and business teams with high positivity ratios are associated with flourishing while those with low positivity ratios are likely to languish.[19]

Family businesses would benefit by being mindful of the importance of praising family and other employees consistently, in accord with the positivity ratio. This is not to suggest that family members should make contrived or insincere comments, nor be excessively positive to the point of insincerity. However, families in which members are mindful about the importance of making three honestly positive comments for every one negative comment will likely realize better family relationships and enhanced bonds of mutual respect.

Steps to Be More Positive

There is no shortage of advice on how to enhance positive emotions in one's life and relationships. Some of the most common recommendations include:

1. **Maintain a Gratitude Journal**. Every day, write down at least three things that you are grateful for. This practice of consciously acknowledging your blessings and all that you have to be grateful for, even small blessings, has been shown to enhance positive emotions.
2. **Reframe Problems as Opportunities**. Describing a circumstance as a problem can zap our energy. Reframing that circumstance as an opportunity can be energizing.
3. **Live a Healthy Lifestyle**. Eat nutritious foods and exercise. Studies suggest that exercising as little as three times a week can help create a more positive mood.
4. **Smile**. Research confirms that smiling can boost happiness.
5. **Surround Yourself with Positive People**. The attitudes of those around us can make a huge difference. Seek out people who are encouraging and optimistic and who make you feel good. Steer clear of negative people who are critical and who make you feel depressed.
6. **Minimize Exposure to Negativity**. Consider limiting the time you spend tracking the news, much of which is filled with depressing stories about matters most of us have no control over. Instead, focus on the positive things in life and on matters you can influence.

A particularly important relationship in a family business is that which exists between a husband and a wife. A lot of research has been conducted on the importance of expressing positive emotions in a marriage. For example, in her article, *The Happy Couple*, author Suzann Pileggi Pawelski notes the following facts:

1. In the past few years, psychologists have discovered that thriving couples accentuate the positive in life more than those who languish or split. They not only cope well during hardship, but also celebrate the happy moments and work to build more into their lives.
2. How couples handle good news may matter even more to their relationship than their ability to support each other under difficult circumstances.
3. Happy couples also experience a higher ratio of upbeat emotions to negative ones than people in unsuccessful pairings.[20]

Is Positivity Always Good?

Epictetus long ago cautioned, "If one oversteps the bounds of moderation, the greatest pleasures cease to please." Such moderation can be appropriate when it comes to the recommendation to be intentionally positive as well. Aside from the risk of being perceived as insincere, it sometimes pays to be concerned. As one observer wrote, "[c]heery thoughts aren't for everyone all the time. Plenty of jobs require anxiety, pessimism, and even fear. . . . Airline pilots facing ice shouldn't be optimistic. Nor should accountants spotting fishy numbers, or regulators probing corruption."[21]

Moreover—and notwithstanding this country's Declaration of Independence (which provides, in relevant part, that "We hold these truths to be self-evident, that all men are created equal, that they are endowed by their Creator with certain unalienable Rights, that among these are Life, Liberty and the pursuit of Happiness)—our focus isn't always appropriately on "happiness." A common example used to highlight this point is that soldiers, fighting for their country, feel a variety of emotions (such as love of country) but not necessarily happiness. Life can be challenging and complicated, and focusing on being positive isn't always appropriate.

On the other hand, creating a positive culture may be the single most important step a family business can take to increase its likelihood of success. Empirical data demonstrates a clear connection between happiness and business success. Most of the time, happy people, whether employers or employees, are better workers than unhappy people.

Consider the following exchange in a recent interview between Gardiner Morse, a senior editor at the *Harvard Business Review* (HBR), and Daniel Gilbert, a Harvard psychology professor and best-selling author of *Stumbling on Happiness*:

> **[Morse/HBR]** Many managers would say that contented people aren't the most productive employees, so you want to keep people a little uncomfortable, maybe a little anxious about their jobs.

> **[Gilbert]** Managers who collect data instead of relying on intuition don't say that. I know of no data showing that anxious, fearful employees are more creative or productive. Remember, contentment doesn't mean sitting and staring at the wall. That's what people do when they are bored, and people hate being bored. We know that people are happiest when they're appropriately challenged—when they're trying to achieve goals that are difficult but not out of reach . . . Psychologists have studied reward and punishment for a century, and the bottom line is perfectly clear: Reward works better.[22]

Focus on Appreciation

I am often struck by how many family members seem to take their family businesses for granted. Rather than appreciating their many blessings, including the chance to work with family, job security, and even wealth, many family members seem to focus on what they perceive to be problems. Family members would benefit from focusing more of their energy on what they have to be grateful for, rather than what they are missing. David L. Cooperrider, professor of social entrepreneurship at the Weatherhead School of Management, is regarded as the father of Appreciative Inquiry (AI), a planning paradigm that seeks to bring out the best in people and their organizations through the systematic discovery of what gives "life" to an organization when it is functioning at its best. AI is based on helping people and organizations flourish by focusing them on the pursuit of opportunities and possibilities through a continuous cycle of improvement, characterized by the following "4 Ds," which are also depicted in Figure 4:

1. **Discovery**: asking people/organizations to identify their best qualities;
2. **Dream**: asking people/organizations to envision their possibilities;
3. **Design**: developing an action plan; and
4. **Destiny/Delivery**: executing the plan.

Figure 4: The 4-D Cycle of Continuous Improvement

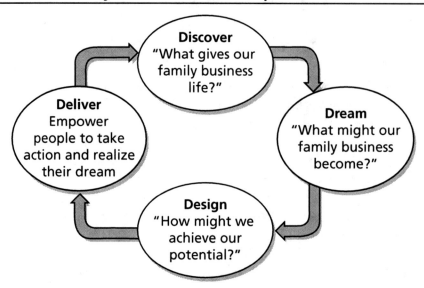

AI is based on several key principles, starting with the fundamental notion that we create our reality by what we choose to focus on. What we focus on, in turn, is a function of what questions we ask. Helping families in business together ask the right questions—those that prompt the most constructive inquiry and discussion—will help increase the likelihood that they can create a positive future. Typical questions that might be used to begin the discovery phase of an AI conversation within a family business could be:

1. What were your hopes and passions when you chose to start or join this family business?
2. Describe a situation related to your family business in which you felt this passion. Where were you at the time? What happened? What made the experience so positive?
3. Describe a "peak experience" or time in which you felt appreciated.
4. Describe a time in which your participation in a family business initiative made a difference.
5. Describe what makes working at your family business unique and rewarding. (What gives "life" to your family business?)
6. What are your family business's best practices?
7. What three wishes do you have to make your family business the best place to work?
8. What three wishes do you have to make your family business the best place for your customers?
9. What three things about your family business are you grateful for?

While a problem-solving approach tends to breed criticism that, in turn, can create arguments and defensiveness ("it wasn't my fault"), applying AI to family business conversations can create constructive conversations based on how to best leverage a family's capabilities, skills, and assets, in order to drive progress and accomplishments.

> *"It could be argued that all leadership is appreciative leadership. It's the capacity to see the best in the world around us, in our colleagues, and in the groups we are trying to lead. It's the capacity to see the most creative and improbable opportunities in the marketplace. It's the capacity to see with an appreciative eye the true and the good, the better and the possible."*[23]
>
> David L. Cooperrider

Unlike some pop psychology suggestions, such as "look in the mirror and tell yourself to 'be happy'" or "the word *impossible* is not in our family business vocabulary," AI is grounded in reality and in the intentional focus on the appreciation of real assets, real skills, real capabilities, and real possibilities. For example, it might be unrealistic for a small family baking business operating in rural New York state to develop a business plan to sell cookies in China the following year. But it could be potentially exciting to think about expanding statewide, or starting to sell additional products that complement the business. Perhaps with the right plan, selling in China would one day become possible. The practice essentially encourages an intentional use of higher-order thinking.

Dr. Dan Baker, writing about Appreciative Inquiry, explains that:

> Finding the right answers starts with asking the right questions. Asking the wrong questions—such as, Why me?—leads nowhere. Or worse.
>
> Because we live in a survival obsessed, fearful culture, we're accustomed to asking the wrong questions. We tend to approach every difficult situation with the basic question of What's wrong? There's a better question: What's right?

Baker continues, noting that, "Negativity has its place. Asking what's wrong can be effective in an emergency. But even then, it's just half of the equation. Nothing ever gets fixed until someone figures out a positive solution."[24]

> I recall bumping into a high school friend a number of years ago and learning that he was getting a divorce. Obviously saddened by that prospect, I asked him if he and his wife had sought counseling. When he replied that they had but that hadn't helped, I asked about the marriage counselor's approach. He shared with me that the counselor had asked them to take a few minutes and write on a piece of paper the top ten problems they had with each other. After creating their respective lists,
>
> *(continued)*

the counselor began to address the problems one at a time. My friend explained how surprised and angry his wife was when they got to problems eight, nine and ten, not previously realizing these were problems. Sadly, my friend acknowledged to me that they weren't big problems, but the assignment was to list ten problems, not seven.

In an interesting contrast, about that time a client came to see me to discuss business-planning opportunities in contemplation of a pending divorce. I discussed AI with my client and asked him to go home and, over dinner that night, talk with his wife about what they saw in each other some years earlier when they decided to get married and how they might recapture that. I'm not a matrimonial lawyer, and my experience is limited and anecdotal, but I am quite proud of the fact that this couple decided to remain married.

While many family businesses have created structures like family councils to promote robust communication, too many of those meetings are approached in traditional problem-solving modes. Ironically, such discussions can create more problems than they resolve. I am aware of families that have come together for family meetings but, when one family member pointed out a problem, another family member, fearing responsibility, became defensive, and soon, the discussion wound up in finger pointing and fighting. Imagine the difference if a family were to come together in an appreciative conversation designed to help them discover their strengths, interests, assets, and skills, and the opportunities and possibilities to build on them.

With practice and effort, our ability to find things to appreciate continues to expand. Consider the following from Vietnamese Buddhist monk Thich Nhat Hanh from his book, *The Heart of the Buddha's Teaching*:

> When we have a toothache, we know that not having a toothache is happiness. But later, when we don't have a toothache, we don't remember our non-toothache. Practicing mindfulness helps us learn to appreciate the well-being that is already there.[25]

Practice Altruism

Unselfish consideration for the welfare of others is good for us and for family businesses. Frequently cited examples of altruistic people include Martin Luther King Jr., who was killed as a result of his efforts to extend basic civil rights in this country, and Mother Teresa, who adhered to her vows of poverty while helping the neediest people in underdeveloped countries throughout her life.

Studies suggest that altruistic behavior can reap tremendous benefits for a family business. Francis Flynn, the Paul E. Holden Professor of Organizational Behavior at Stanford University's Graduate School of Business, studied 161 engineers working for a telecommunications firm in California. The engineers were individually responsible for helping to resolve engineering problems sent in from around the country. Professor Flynn asked each engineer to report on how often they helped other engineers and the value provided through their exchanges. Part of what he was interested in learning was how one-sidedly generous the engineers were. He also asked employees to rate how highly they regarded one another.

Professor Flynn found that:

1. Employees who generously help their colleagues but get little in exchange are well-regarded by colleagues;
2. Employees who generously help their colleagues but do not receive help in exchange are less productive; and
3. Employees who both generously receive and give help are relatively more productive, particularly those who help each other most often.[26]

In short, a culture of frequent giving and receiving boosts both productivity and social standing. Professor Flynn's conclusions are consistent with the observation that humans were able to evolve, in part, by acting altruistically. As a result, altruism has become part of our nature. As Larry Arnhart noted:

> Cooperation within a group of individuals can arise whenever it benefits all members of the group, so long as the cheaters who refuse to contribute their fair share can be identified and punished. Even in very large groups, *having a reputation for being cooperative can confer great benefits, which thus fosters cooperative behavior.*[27]

The benefits of altruism will be further considered in chapter 8 when we discuss the application of game theory to resolving disputes in family businesses.

Ongoing studies suggest that corporate commitment to assisting the community at large greatly increases employee motivation, strengthens the positive reputation of the company, and increases profits. Michael Porter and Mark Kramer observe that assisting the community is even a key to a business's continuing success. Writing in *Harvard Business Review,* Professors Porter and Kramer note that companies often remain trapped in an outdated approach to value creation by which they seek to optimize short-term financial performance while ignoring customer needs. Acknowledging that "[t]he presumed trade-offs between economic efficiency and social progress have been institutionalized in

(continued)

decades of policy choices," Professors Porter and Kramer suggest that companies can not only continue to prosper but that they can do so by focusing on how to create economic value in a way that also addresses society's needs and challenges. They write that:

> Businesses must reconnect company success with social progress. Shared value is not social responsibility, philanthropy, or even sustainability, but a new way to achieve economic success. It is not on the margin of what companies do but at the center. We believe that it can give rise to the next major transformation of business thinking.[28]

In *Altruism, Happiness, and Health: It's Good to Be Good*, Stephen G. Post, a member of the Department of Bioethics, School of Medicine, Case Western Reserve University, writes that:

> Altruistic emotions can gain dominance over anxiety and fear, turning off the fight-flight response. Immediate and unspecified physiological changes may occur as a result of volunteering and helping others, leading to the so-called helper's high.[29]

Martin Seligman describes developing evidence of the causal connection between altruism and becoming happier, noting how he gave to one of his classes an assignment to do two activities, one that was "enjoyable" and one that was "philanthropic," and then write about the difference in how the students felt afterward. The students reported that "the positive effects of the philanthropic activities were much longer lasting."[30] While further studies are needed, existing empirical data suggests that family members who help other family members will feel better for having helped, and will help their business as well.

Another study, perhaps particularly relevant for families in business together, suggests the importance of parents acting as role models for their children by behaving altruistically.[31] A recurring theme in the literature is how positive emotions beget positive emotions. Family businesses would be well served to find ways to help each other, their employees, and their communities through philanthropy and volunteerism. By embracing altruism as a core value and structuring a work environment that encourages such behavior, families should expect to both feel better *and* enhance their odds of working together successfully.

Practice Civility

Familiarity can sometimes make it easier for a family member to treat other family members worse than he or she would treat nonfamily members, such as by teasing, criticizing, behaving rudely, or simply taking them for granted. Common courtesies typically shown to a stranger are often not shown to family members. Over time, it is possible that such bad behavior can gradually and almost imperceptibly escalate, creating a culture of incivility.

In a recent book, *The Cost of Bad Behavior: How Incivility Is Damaging Your Business and What to Do About It*, Professors Christine Pearson and Christine Porath report that workplace incivility can severely affect a business and its bottom line.[32] They observe that incivility's measurable costs alone are enormous. Job stress, for instance, costs U.S. corporations $300 billion a year, much of which has been shown to stem from workplace incivility. They also note that:

> half of employees who had experienced uncivil behavior at work intentionally decreased their efforts. More than a third deliberately decreased the quality of their work. Two-thirds spent a lot of time avoiding the offender, and about the same number said their performance had declined. . . . Incivility prevents people from thriving.[33]

Professors Pearson and Porath observe that incivility's true impact stretches far beyond that which is measurable in dollar value and includes the damage resulting from increased employee turnover, the disruption of work teams, and the decline of helpful behavior.[34] For example, they note:

- 53 percent of employees surveyed lost work time worrying about an incident and future interactions with the offender.
- 28 percent lost work time trying to avoid the offender.
- 37 percent reported a weakened sense of commitment to their organization.
- 22 percent reduced their efforts at work.
- 10 percent decreased the amount of time they spent at work.
- 46 percent thought about changing their jobs—to get away from the offender.
- 12 percent actually changed jobs.[35]

Companies like Microsoft, Cisco, and Starbucks have focused on eliminating incivility in the workplace, and have saved millions of dollars in doing so. These companies have programs that seek to structurally support good behavior, such as by rewarding employees who exemplify great behavior while holding badly behaving employees accountable. Many successful companies are also sending managers to leadership programs and seminars to enhance their relationship skills.

Sue Shellenbarger, a columnist for the *Wall Street Journal*, wrote an article titled "Showing Appreciation at the Office? No, Thanks," in which she reports on the research confirming that employees who feel appreciated "are more productive and loyal."[36] Unfortunately, the research also suggests that the workplace ranked last among places people express gratitude. In spite of the fact that showing appreciation cuts turnover and increases profits, people find it easier to blame than to say thank you.

Following are some common ways that family businesses might combat incivility.

1. Establish and enforce policies that spell out the unacceptability of incivility.
2. Encourage family members to consider the impact of their words and actions on others before acting.
3. Identify ways in which individual differences can be used as strengths to help the family business succeed.
4. Demonstrate genuine interest in everyone throughout the organization.
5. Model civility.
6. Screen job candidates to avoid hiring negative influences.
7. Provide employees and family members with continuing education to learn how to better manage difficult people.
8. Solicit anonymous feedback to help identify bad behavior.

> I'm pleased to note that the legal profession has taken note of the importance of civility in professional practice. Various initiatives, including Continuing Legal Education programs, are underway to make the practice of law more civil. Sean Carter, a 1992 graduate of the Harvard Law School and founder of Lawpsided Seminars, delivers seminars across the country on a variety of topics, including my favorite, *Nice Lawyers Finish First: Acquiring the Seven Virtues of Good Lawyering*. The seven virtues that Carter discusses are chastity, temperance, charity, diligence, patience, kindness, and humility.

Be Supportive

A corollary to the proposition that families benefit from treating each other positively is that families also benefit from being supportive of each other. Changing the paradigm from criticizing someone who made a mistake to pointing out the lesson to be taken from an experience can be significant. Interestingly, employees who behave more like teachers than critics also tend to benefit from their constructive approach. Research has shown that employees who provide the most social support are 40 percent more likely to receive a promotion in the following year, report significantly higher job satisfaction, and feel ten times more engaged by their jobs than people who fall in the lowest quartile of providing social support.[37]

One way to be supportive is to help people stop dwelling on negative events or problems, while encouraging and helping them to pay more attention to positive developments, opportunities, and possibilities instead. Ironically, traditional therapy can actually encourage a "negative focus." Family members, particularly leaders, would be wise to consider how they might help shift stakeholders' focus to the positive aspects of the family's business—the possibilities and opportunities that can realistically be pursued and, in so doing, help the business grow and prosper. For example, conversation can be steered to discussing what went right during the day, or how progress on an initiative was made. Another suggestion is to encourage family members to supplement the to-do list with an "I did it" list, to give sharper perspective on accomplishments and progress.

Companies benefit when managers show interest in an employee's personal life or demonstrate real concern about an employee's family needs.[38] Further, employees with managers trained in supporting a flexible workplace had better physical health, were more satisfied with their jobs, and experienced less turnover than those employees whose managers did not have this training.[39]

Learn to Forgive

Being human means that we will all make mistakes. Indeed, our greatest lessons often are the result of our biggest mistakes. As family businesses are not safe havens from the slings and arrows of humanity, there is ample opportunity to hurt someone else's feelings or self-esteem. If family members can't find a way to move past that hurt, instead of harboring resentment and animosity, their business will struggle to survive. No one wins a battle of egos in a family business.

Religion has long counseled us to let go of any resentment.[40] So too have great philosophers. One well-known and oft-cited quotation is Alexander Pope's observation that "To err is human; to forgive, divine."[41] Science now confirms that forgiving—the intentional choice to let go of any resentment we feel as a result of having been harmed by another—may be one of the healthiest and smartest things we can do for ourselves. It may also be one of the most important qualities enabling families to succeed from generation to generation.

One of the more interesting initiatives on how the act of forgiveness can be helpful is The Forgiveness Project at Stanford University, headed by Dr. Frederic Luskin. Among other benefits, such as reducing stress, his research shows that as people learn to forgive, they become more hopeful and optimistic. His work suggests that the act of forgiving is a key aspect of rebuilding and maintaining trust in the workplace and helping family members to move forward effectively.[42]

Because we are all taught the importance of forgiving but don't always know how to forgive, Dr. Luskin offers the following nine-step plan:

Step 1: Clarify your feelings about what happened that you found unacceptable.

Step 2: Recognize that forgiveness can help you, not just the person you are forgiving.

Step 3: Understand that your goal is to find peace.

Step 4: Recognize that your hurt feelings, thoughts, and any physical upset you are experiencing are due to how your brain continues to process what happened in the past, not what is happening in the present.

Step 5: At the moment you feel upset, practice the use of a simple stress-management technique to soothe your body's flight-or-fight response.

Step 6: Stop expecting things from other people.

Step 7: Instead of mentally replaying the events that led up to your hurt, focus your energy into accomplishing one of your positive goals.

Step 8: Remember that a life well lived is your best revenge.

Step 9: Rewrite your grievance story to remind you of the power you have to create a better story.[43]

By choosing to forgive, an individual does not necessarily need to excuse the wrongdoer. It is simply a choice to stop feeling angry at someone who has wronged us by looking forward at what the possibilities in the future offer instead of backward at actions and choices that cannot be changed. Forgiving is not always easy. Our brains tend to dwell on hurtful events that only reinforce negative emotions and corresponding fight-or-flight behavior like getting even. Because it is difficult for our brains to be both positive and negative at the same time, these negative feelings tend to crowd out positive feelings, making it difficult to get past feelings of hurt. Aside from creating unhealthy physiological reactions in our bodies, such negativity can make ongoing working relationships within a family business unworkable. While we'll discuss other dispute resolution mechanisms in chapter 8, often the most effective way to resolve a dispute is for one party to apologize for committing a wrong and the other party to accept the apology and offer forgiveness. If parties are unable to move past hurt from wrongs suffered, family business failure is inevitable. It is usually better to simply move on.

Be Compassionate

I often find myself reminiscing about a trip to a local drugstore with my father, a beloved physician in Buffalo, New York. I was a teenager at the time and anxious to buy what we needed so that I could get to whatever it was I was planning on doing. My agenda was interrupted, however, when my father bumped into one of his patients in the store. They proceeded to take several minutes talking about some medical issues affecting a member of this person's family. Annoyed with the unexpected interruption, while we were driving home, I asked my father how he controlled himself when being bothered on his personal time. He quickly answered that he never felt like he was being bothered. He explained that life can be hard, and that he had great compassion for his patients and was always happy to talk about someone's medical concerns.

Over the years, I have found myself reflecting on that conversation and, as I continue to study families and family businesses, I think that there may be no virtue more important than compassion. Unlike empathy, which describes an emotional, yet passive, understanding or sensitivity to how another feels, compassion moves beyond trying to feel someone's emotional pain by trying to do something about it. Sometimes hugging a family member or friend and asking "How can I help?" can make a world of difference. Establishing and maintaining good relationships with workplace colleagues by acting compassionately can help foster a collegial atmosphere that enables everyone to work well together. Compassion facilitates our insight and understanding about why our family, friends, and workplace colleagues behave as they do. For example, a colleague might appear to be angry with you in the morning when, in fact, he lost sleep the night before because he was up all night with a sick child. Imagine the goodwill created by a compassionate colleague who, knowing that a coworker has a sick child at home, says, "Go home. I can handle the work today."

Scientists have been studying the impact of compassion and the results, consistent with the findings about other higher-order emotions, again suggest that the great philosophers and religions had it right when they encouraged us to live compassionate lives.

I suspect that people who sincerely try to help someone who is hurting experience a variety of positive emotions that bring the realization that they are helping themselves as well.

Compassion in a Family Business

Practicing compassion in the workplace can have a dramatic impact, particularly in a family business where individuals face a variety of unique family challenges, such as sibling rivalry and estate tax concerns—which only adds to the stress resulting from "workday challenges."[44] Like other people, family members may experience stress from the loss of a loved one, an argument at home, or the illness of family, friends, and colleagues. Encouraging compassion at work has the capacity to change feelings and expectations with many positive consequences. Studies show that actively engaging employees at all levels to respond to the needs of others in a positive way reduces employee stress while promoting teamwork and creative problem solving. Moreover, workplaces that exhibit compassion generally have higher rates of satisfaction and higher rates of loyalty. Consider the difference in employee morale (and engagement) if a boss pays a visit to the home of an employee who has just suffered a personal loss, perhaps the death of a parent, spouse, or child, with another workforce where the boss never acknowledges the loss, publicly or privately.

The few extra moments taken by an employer to show compassion can make a world of difference to an organization as a whole. Simple acts of compassion reverberate across the entire company.

Conclusion

It is now widely accepted that a positive culture is a bigger factor behind employee job satisfaction than compensation and is more often the reason that employees remain at their jobs with great attitudes that directly enhance operational performance. The impact of a positive culture on enhancing intra-family trust is reflected in Figure 5. The field of positive psychology continues to develop and there is much work that remains to be done. The suggestions set forth above are only a few examples of how the findings from this burgeoning field can yield great dividends to family businesses by helping counteract the adverse effects of a negative culture. I am confident that this field offers the framework to help families in business work together in a constructive fashion, helping to ensure that they have taken the first step toward long-term success.

Figure 5: The Impact of Success Factor 1—Positive Culture

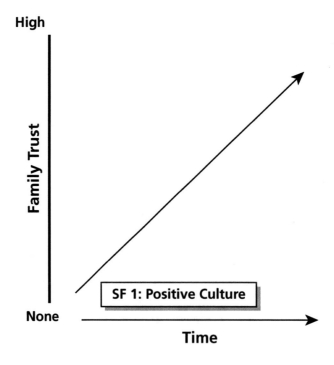

Quotations

"Be kind, for everyone you meet is fighting a hard battle."

Plato

"Even the rich are hungry for love, for being cared for, for being wanted, for having someone to call their own."

Mother Teresa

"I have found the paradox, that if you love until it hurts, there can be no more hurt, only more love."

Mother Teresa

"An eye for an eye makes the whole world blind."

Mahatma Gandhi

"Forgiveness does not change the past, but it does enlarge the future."

Paul Boese

"All major religious traditions carry basically the same message, that is love, compassion and forgiveness . . . the important thing is they should be part of our daily lives."

Dalai Lama

"We often think of peace as the absence of war; that if the powerful countries would reduce their arsenals, we could have peace. But if we look deeply into the weapons, we see our own minds—our prejudices, fears, and ignorance . . . Seek to become more aware of what causes anger and separation, and what overcomes them. Root out the violence in your life, and learn to live compassionately and mindfully."

Thich Nhat Hanh

Enhancing Job Fit and Happiness | 4

"I have found the best way to give advice to your children is to find out what they want and then advise them to do it."

Harry S. Truman

Background: Failure Factor 2 (The Subordination of Fit to Convenience)

While the previous chapter explored the imperative for families to establish and maintain a positive culture in their businesses through healthy and constructive interpersonal relationships, cultivating a positive culture also requires that individual family members feel satisfied and fulfilled with their roles in the business.

Sadly, such positive feelings may be lacking when family members join the business because of family expectations or because doing so seems to be the easiest path to a job. Decisions borne out of such personal or family convenience tend to result in having family members who, faced with job expectations and demands that are ill-suited for their skills and interests, become frustrated and unhappy. This leads to behaviors or performance that can create family-wide disappointment, resentment, and stress. Ultimately and inexorably those negative feelings and behaviors lead to infighting and conflict.

Career choices based on pursuing such family business opportunities are consistent with this country's long-held view that happiness can best be pursued by striving to secure the financial rewards that accompany success. We are prone to think this will ultimately secure our happiness.

Our longtime cultural focus on making money so that we can one day become happy is contrary to great bodies of timeless wisdom. As we'll explore, contemporary wisdom borne from scientifically derived empirical data also establishes how individuals in business are more likely to be happy and successful when they pursue career paths that maximize their ability to use their unique skills, talents, interests, and passions.

Antidotes to Failure Factor 2, the subordination of job fit to convenience, can be found in many places, including philosophy, spirituality, religion, and ethics. Accordingly, rather than simply recapitulating general advice and suggestions on happiness and living life well, this chapter focuses specifically on the science behind why promoting fit over convenience and money is an essential ingredient to the success of a family business. Practical suggestions for what individuals and families can do to help enhance fit for individuals and organizations are also offered below.

> There isn't, of course, one "definitive list" of what one needs to be happy, and everyone, undoubtedly would have their own unique and distinctly personal thoughts on the subject. Religious figures, philosophers, psychologists, and self-help writers do tend, however, to recognize many of the same core qualities that happy people share, including those set forth in chapter 3 (e.g., altruism, compassion, appreciation, etc.). In *Secrets from the Delphi Café: Unlocking the Code to Happiness*, Bob Rich and I took a stab at the subject, writing about a mythical waitress, Sophie, who helps one of her customers discover that being happy requires each individual to maintain a Healthy lifestyle, be Appreciative, pursue interests that one is Passionate about, be Patient, and retain a sense of Youthful curiosity as one ages.

Why Does Happiness Matter?

Before continuing any further, I think it would be helpful to consider *why* businesses should care about whether their employees are happy. I gave a speech in Southern California in the early 1990s to a group of successful family business owners. Addressing such subjects as culture, values, and emotional intelligence, I found myself looking around at my audience and getting the sense that those who hadn't fallen asleep couldn't wait for me to finish. It was a long way to travel from Buffalo, New York, to hear from my audience (all of whom were men and, as I recall, generally members of the "senior generation") that they really didn't have time to focus on the "soft issues." According to them, business and financial decisions were what drove their company's success and they couldn't be bothered with, as one member of the audience called it, my "milk and granola" advice.

Times have changed and the business world has come a long way in recognizing that having happy employees and stakeholders is an essential element to enhancing the corporate bottom line. For example, the *Wall Street Journal* printed a lead article on what to do "When the Boss Is a Screamer." That article, noting that the "yelling boss" is a vestige of earlier days, reports that:

> The new consensus among managers is that yelling alarms people, drives them away rather than inspiring them, and hurts the quality of their work.
>
> . . . While underlings may work hard for difficult bosses, hoping for a shred of praise, few employees do their best work amid yelling. Verbal aggression tends to impair victims' working memory, reducing their ability to understand instructions and perform such basic tasks as operating a computer.[1]

The business press and many enlightened workplaces are increasingly coming to realize that the fear created by an angry boss only puts employees in counterproductive fight-or-flight mode and is bad for business. In his best-selling book *The Positive Dog*, author Jon Gordon describes how a positive culture creates powerful and demonstrable benefits to both a business and its stakeholders. Figure 6 captures Gordon's comparison and contrasts of some of the personal costs of being negative against some of the countervailing benefits of being positive:

Figure 6: The Cost-Benefit Analysis of Negativity versus Positivity

The Costs of Negativity	The Benefits of Positivity
1. Ninety percent of doctor visits are stress related, according to the Centers for Disease Control and Prevention.	1. Positive people live longer. In a study of nuns, those who regularly expressed positive emotions lived an average of ten years longer than those who didn't.
2. A study found that negative employees might scare off every customer they speak with.[2]	2. Positive, optimistic salespeople sell more than pessimistic salespeople.
3. At work, too many negative interactions can decrease the productivity of a team, according to Barbara Frederickson's research at the University of Michigan.	3. Those working in positive work environments outperform those in negative work environments.

(continued)

The Costs of Negativity	The Benefits of Positivity
4. Negativity affects the morale, performance, and productivity of teams.	4. Positive leaders are able to make better decisions under pressure.
5. One negative person can create a miserable office environment for everyone else.	5. Marriages are much more likely to succeed when the couple experiences a 5-to-1 ratio of positive to negative interactions.
6. Robert Cross's research at the University of Virginia demonstrates that 90 percent of anxiety at work is created by 5 percent of one's network.	6. Positive people who regularly express positive emotions are more resilient when facing stress, challenges, and adversity.
7. Negative emotions are associated with decreased life span and longevity.	7. Positive people are able to maintain a broader perspective and see the big picture, which helps them identify solutions.
8. Negative emotions increase the risk of heart attack and stroke.	8. Positive thoughts and emotions counter the negative effects of stress. For example, you can't be thankful and stressed at the same time.
9. Negativity is associated with greater stress, less energy, and more pain.	9. Positive emotions such as gratitude and appreciation help athletes perform at a higher level.
10. Negative people have fewer friends.[3]	10. Positive people have more friends, which is a key factor of happiness and longevity.
	11. Positive and popular leaders are more likely to garner the support of others and receive pay raises and promotions and achieve greater success in the workplace.[4]

These and similar findings highlight the need for family business planning to include an intentional focus on seeking to maximize employee happiness. Clearly, organizations are better off having happy employees. One of the best ways to accomplish this objective is to focus on creating a good fit between family members as prospective employees and the business. Good fits result in happy and productive employees; poor fits do not.

Shawn Achor, one of the world's leading experts on human potential, writes:

> More than a decade of groundbreaking research in the fields of positive psychology and neuroscience has proven in no uncertain terms that . . . happiness is the precursor to success, not merely the result. And that happiness and optimism actually *fuel* performance and achievement. . . .
>
> Waiting to be happy limits our brain's potential for success, whereas cultivating positive brains makes us more motivated, efficient, resilient, creative, and productive, which drives performance upward. This discovery has been confirmed by thousands of scientific studies . . . [5]

Finding Happiness by Pursuing Our Calling

While I'm sure everyone has their own unique sense of what they mean by "happiness in the workplace," the famous psychologist Abraham Maslow might have most eloquently captured my sense of the concept when he wrote that "the most beautiful fate, the most wonderful good fortune that can happen to any human being, is to be paid for doing that which he passionately loves to do."

Many of history's greatest and most respected thinkers have long encouraged the pursuit of what we passionately love to do—work that gives us so much meaning and is so rewarding that it is often simply referred to as our "calling." I have long been inspired by Henry David Thoreau's oft-quoted dictum that "if one advances confidently in the direction of his dreams, and endeavors to live the life which he has imagined, he will meet with a success unexpected in common hours."

Abraham Maslow suggested that people are motivated in accordance with a "hierarchy of needs," each one of which needs to be fulfilled before moving on to other, more advanced needs. Most often displayed as a pyramid, the most basic needs are our physical requirements for food, water, sleep, safety, and security. As people progress up the pyramid, needs for love, friendship, self-esteem, and feelings of accomplishment become increasingly important. At the peak of the pyramid, Maslow placed the importance of self-actualization, a process of growing and developing in order to achieve individual potential. His model helps explain why earning incremental amounts of income provides only minimal enhancements to happiness. That is why billionaires aren't necessarily happier than middle-income earners. Money doesn't buy happiness; self-actualization does.

Beyond simply helping us to better appreciate the distinctions between what we might refer to as a "job," a "career," or a "calling," scientists have given us tools to help us understand the difference by expanding the knowledge that informs us how to be happier and more successful.

Our understanding of these differences arises because many psychologists were historically interested in better appreciating the relationship between nature, nurture, and happiness. Psychologists like Freud viewed personality as a characteristic that was shaped in childhood by family environment. As scientists learned more about the human genome, there was an increased appreciation for the relationship between our genetic makeup and individual happiness. Many psychologists now believe that our happiness is a function of both our genetic makeup and our environment. Jonathan Haidt, a professor of psychology at the University of Virginia, notes that one of the most important ideas in positive psychology is the articulation by three psychologists (Sonja Lyubomirsky, Ken Sheldon, and David Schkade) that, "[t]he level of happiness that you actually experience (H) is determined by your biological set point (S) plus the conditions of your life (C) plus the voluntary activities (V) you do."[6] This "happiness formula" can be set forth as follows:

$$H = S + C + V$$

While we are not able to control all of the elements in this formula, of particular importance is how each of us has the power to control our voluntary activities—the V in the happiness formula. Specifically, we all have a degree of choice to pursue our calling instead of just getting a job because it is lucrative or convenient.

Martin Seligman writes that he "actually detest[s] the word happiness, which is so overused that it has become almost meaningless." He believes the word "is an unworkable term for science, or for any practical goal such as education, therapy, public policy, or just changing your personal life."[7] Seligman continues, noting that the problem with the word "happiness" is

> not only that it underexplains what we choose but that the modern ear immediately hears 'happy' to mean buoyant mood, merriment, good cheer, and smiling. . . . 'Happiness' historically is not closely tied to such hedonics—feeling cheerful or merry is a far cry from what Thomas Jefferson declared that we have a right to pursue—and it is an even further cry from my intentions for a positive psychology.[8]

As a solution to this ongoing definitional problem, Seligman suggests that the focus of positive psychology should be on "well-being," not "happiness."[9]

It may be that the "happiness" construct is too deeply engrained in our thinking, culture, and literature for that to happen. While Seligman and others continue to inform our understanding of how to live a fulfilling life, I suspect that we're stuck with the word "happy"—a word that we will all continue to use, define, and experience in our own personal and unique way.

Identifying Our Calling

Mihaly Csikszentmihalyi, a professor of psychology at the University of Chicago, writing in his best-selling book *Flow: The Psychology of Optimal Experience*, describes the research behind the proposition that "happiness is not something that happens . . . Happiness, in fact, is a condition that must be prepared for, cultivated, and defended privately by each person."[10]

Intending to describe absorption in a task that's appropriately challenging (neither so easy that we get bored nor so difficult that we get frustrated), Csikszentmihalyi uses the term "flow" to capture the sense of effortless action people experience in moments when they feel as if they are functioning at their very best, or "in the zone." As our skills increase, the complexity of our challenges should increase as well so that we avoid becoming bored. He captures the dynamic nature of flow in the following diagram, Figure 7:

Figure 7: Flow: Optimizing Experience through Fit[11]

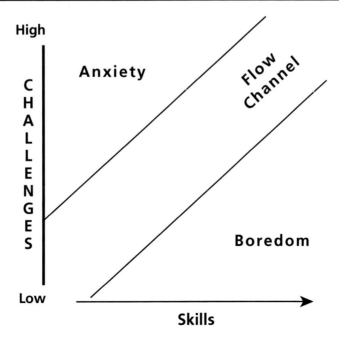

Finding flow is, in short, a function of an individual balancing her skill and abilities against the optimum level of challenges and demands so that there is a sense of excitement and control or "choice." The following steps can help enhance the achievement of flow:

1. Work on tasks that you have a chance of completing.
2. Concentrate on what you are doing.
3. Ensure the task has clear goals.
4. Receive immediate feedback.
5. Ensure the activity demands a deep but effortless involvement, removing from awareness the worries of everyday life.
6. Ensure the activity allows you to exercise a sense of control over your actions.

While in flow, concern for oneself disappears and the sense of duration of time is altered; hours pass by in what might seem like minutes.[12]

Psychologist Ed Diener has demonstrated that the frequency of one's positive experiences is a better predictor of happiness than the intensity.[13] Given that a typical employee works at least 40 hours a week, having a job that is a good fit may be one of the best steps anyone could take to increase their happiness. The corollary to Diener's findings, of course, is that having a job one dislikes is the root cause of much unhappiness.

Action Opportunities for Family Businesses to Enhance Flow

Csikszentmihalyi's work has great implications for family businesses. Instead of choosing to work in the family business because of status, convenience, or money, family members are much more likely to be happy and successful if they choose to work in a position that allows them to maximize the time they spend using their unique skills and talents for the challenges and opportunities they face.

Steve Jobs famously offered this recommendation at a commencement address he delivered at Stanford University when he advised the graduates that:

[our] time is limited, so don't waste it living someone else's life. Don't be trapped by dogma—which is living with the results of other people's thinking. Don't let the noise of others' opinions drown out your own inner voice. And most important, have the courage to follow your heart and intuition. They somehow already know what you truly want to become. Everything else is secondary.[14]

Empirical findings in the field of psychology supporting such recommendations are well documented. Tom Rath has most recently written *StrengthsFinder*

2.0 to share the results of the Gallup organization's continuing research involving more than 10 million people on the topic of employee engagement. Rath, summarizing the results of this research, notes:

> Across the board, having the opportunity to develop our strengths is more important to our success than our role, our title, or even our pay. In this increasingly talent-driven society, we need to know and develop our strengths to figure out where we fit in.[15]

He continues by noting that more than 70 percent of the people surveyed (more than 7 million people) are not focusing on what they do best. Describing the consequences, he writes:

> What happens when you're not in the "strengths zone?" You're quite simply a very different person. In the workplace, you are *six times* less likely to be engaged in your job. When you're not able to use your strengths at work, chances are that you:
>
> - dread going to work;
> - have more negative than positive interactions with your colleagues;
> - treat customers poorly;
> - tell your friends what a miserable company you work for;
> - achieve less on a daily basis; and
> - have fewer positive and creative moments.[16]

Marcus Buckingham and Don Clifton's *Now, Discover Your Strengths* reinforces these insights, explaining that great organizations must not only accommodate the fact that each employee is different, but they must capitalize on these differences.[17] The application of this insight is critical to a family business's efforts to succeed. Families would better serve their businesses and their members by helping them to identify their unique talents as well as a platform, whether inside or outside the family business, where those talents can be pursued.

A variety of empirically validated assessments can be used to help family businesses determine whether a prospective employee (family member or not) would be a good fit for a particular position. These assessments can give helpful feedback on such factors as whether the applicant (1) would work well in the company's culture; (2) has the right education and experience to excel in a position; (3) shares the company's core values; and (4) would have the opportunity to utilize his or her strengths in a prospective position. In my experience, employers who use such assessments tend to do much better in identifying employees who are happy and productive in their work.

(continued)

Oft-used assessments include the Gallup's StrengthsFinder®, Workplace Big Five Profile®, Watson Glaser Critical Thinking Appraisal®, The Bar-On EQ®, Hogan Values®, and the DISC Profile®. Many of these assessments can be completed in less than 15 minutes and can offer very comprehensive and helpful insights that family members can share with each other to help better appreciate each other's personality profiles.

Self-Management

Beyond all these explicit benefits to individuals who experience positive emotions as well as the increasingly obvious correlation to business success, there is an even more important benefit to being happy. The evidence is overwhelming that there is a cumulative buildup of stress hormones when we are in fight-or-flight mode. If not properly metabolized over time, fear-based stress can lead to a variety of health problems such as high blood pressure, chronic fatigue, depression, and susceptibility to infection. In short, evidence suggests that we should shift our current stress-management paradigm to a self-management paradigm, where decisions made and actions taken are more consistent with a healthy and balanced lifestyle.

Another aspect of self-management is training ourselves to slow down and think instead of rushing to judgment, to base decisions on rational thought rather than instinct and intuition. Since we cannot always trust our intuition, Professor Daniel Kahneman suggests that we must learn how to tap into the benefits of what he refers to as "slow thinking."[18] Professor Kahneman observes that emotions continue to play a large role in our decision making and that many executive decisions are guided by instinctual liking or disliking. Successful family business owners must be aware of this fact, and counter it with rational "slow thinking."[19]

Most of the serious thinkers on the subject of happiness seem to agree that happiness is an emotional by-product of living life well.

Conclusion

As a result of "money first" decisions, many family businesses become overcrowded with family members who, for one reason or another, simply aren't good fits in the company. Success in business requires hard work and focus. Those family members who don't naturally fit well in the company's operations often don't work out. The natural result of creating an ecosystem that includes some family members who fit well and others who don't often results in increased frustration, errors, omissions, and negative attitudes from those who participated only for the money, the convenience, or the stature associated with the family business.

Csikszentmihalyi's flow model helps explain why the most successful family businesses are the ones that have rules of participation designed to ensure that family members who go to work in the business are allowed to follow their calling every day, spending as much time as possible in "flow." While I enjoy many great quotations, my favorite "family business" quotation is the one at the start of this chapter by Harry Truman: "I have found the best way to give advice to your children is to find out what they want and then advise them to do it." It is just that simple.

Effective family business planning includes having family members assessed for their strengths, which helps identify whether there is a good fit between the family member and the family business and, if so, what that is. As Professor Csikszentmihalyi observes, "the more a job inherently resembles a game—with variety, appropriate and flexible challenges, clear goals, and immediate feedback—the more enjoyable it will be regardless of the worker's level of development."[20] Family businesses would be wise to encourage career opportunities for family members with this admonition, rather than fostering poor job fits by focusing on irrelevant criteria such as title, prestige, authority—and money. The importance of focusing on ensuring "good job fits" in the workplace is Success Factor 2, and its impact is reflected in Figure 8.

Figure 8: The Impact of Success Factor 2—Good Job Fit

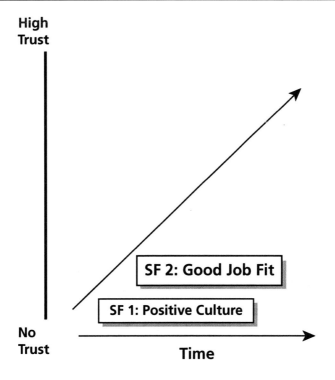

The goals that family members might seek to achieve in their individual pursuit of happiness must, of course, align with the goals of the family business. Otherwise, everyone's individual interests will likely create organizational chaos that, over time, will increase the odds that a business won't successfully transition from generation to generation. For those family members whose goals and interests don't align with the goals of the business, it is much better to recognize that and find constructive ways to allow those individuals to pursue their personal goals and dreams outside of the family business.

Family members also need to appreciate the importance of communicating effectively and the challenges in doing so. In the next chapter, we will turn to why both communications and the alignment around goals and core principles are so important to family business success, and to new strategies to help ensure such an alignment.

On August 19, 2012, Federal Reserve Chairman Ben Bernanke, speaking at a conference of the International Association for Research in Income and Wealth, added his name to the long list of people who believe that we should measure prosperity in terms of happiness and life satisfaction, not just by dollars and with financial statements. Bernanke suggested that the ultimate purpose of economics is "to understand and promote the enhancement of well-being."[21]

Quotations

"What we really want to do is what we are really meant to do. When we do what we are meant to do, money comes to us, doors open for us, we feel useful, and the work we do feels like play to us."

Julia Cameron

"Find something you love to do and you'll never have to work a day in your life."

Harvey MacKay

"Happiness is not in the mere possession of money; it lies in the joy of achievement, in the thrill of creative effort."

Franklin D. Roosevelt

"Genuine happiness consists in those spiritual qualities of love, compassion, patience, tolerance and forgiveness and so on. For it is these which provide both for our happiness and others' happiness."

The Dalai Lama

"Love is the master key that opens the gates of happiness."

Oliver Wendell Holmes

"'Well,' said Pooh, 'what I like best,' and then he had to stop and think. Because although Eating Honey was a very good thing to do, there was a moment just before you began to eat it which was better than when you were, but he didn't know what it was called."

A.A. Milne

"Happiness is like a butterfly which, when pursued, is always beyond our grasp, but, if you will sit down quietly, may alight upon you."

Nathaniel Hawthorne

"Most folks are about as happy as they make up their minds to be."

Abraham Lincoln

"We tend to forget that happiness doesn't come as a result of getting something we don't have, but rather of recognizing and appreciating what we do have."

Frederick Keonig

"Happiness is not a goal; it is a by-product."

Eleanor Roosevelt

"We are no longer happy so soon as we wish to be happier."

Walter Savage Landor

"Ask yourself whether you are happy and you cease to be so."

John Stuart Mill, *Autobiography*, 1873

"There is no way to happiness—happiness is the way."

Thich Nhat Hanh

"Happiness is when what you think, what you say, and what you do are in harmony."

Mahatma Gandhi

Improving Communication through Humility | 5

Background: Failure Factor 3 (Imperfect Communication)

Communication is the lifeblood of a family business's ability to successfully execute its strategy and advance its mission and vision by:

- allowing for the sharing of information, ideas, and core principles;
- facilitating the identification and assessment of new opportunities, strategies, and tactics;
- defining various rules relating to operations; and
- providing the mechanism to give performance feedback and suggestions.

Ample evidence establishes the importance of the quality of communication to a company's prospects for success or failure. Communication has a special role in shaping culture because it is the *tool* by which messages are sent and received. As a tool, communication can be used to build a motivated team in pursuit of common objectives, or it can lead to misunderstanding, frustration, and job dissatisfaction.

For a variety of reasons, communication is rarely easy and misunderstandings occur with unexpected frequency. I'm sure we can all recall an instance where we unintentionally put our foot in our mouth, saying the wrong thing at the wrong time, sometimes without even being aware of our faux pas until someone calls it to our attention. Even large corporations with substantial resources available struggle to be effective communicators. An example of corporate miscommunication is that of Scandinavian vacuum manufacturer Electrolux, for its use of the slogan "Nothing Sucks like an Electrolux" in its United States marketing campaign. One of many more such examples is American Airlines' advertisement of its new leather first-class seats in the Mexican market using the phrase "vuela en cuero," which means "fly naked" in Spanish.

Communication occurs in context, not in isolation. The context of communication within a family business can be even more complicated than in other businesses because of the multiple, differing, and overlapping styles, roles, interests, and relationships that family members might have in the business and in the family. These, in turn, are layered on top of a family's unique history and culture in all its richness, complexity, and emotion. A few of the many factors that contribute to the complexity of communication within a family business include:

1. Unlike in other businesses where communication takes place during working hours, communication within a family business regularly takes place on off hours, including over meals, on weekends, and on holidays;
2. The dynamics of an individual's roles and experience within his or her family is typically irrelevant in most businesses but exert a powerful influence within a family business;
3. Employees in other businesses can stop working, change jobs, and get a fresh start, but a family member who changes jobs doesn't stop being a family member. Tensions might not easily disappear with a change in employment; and
4. Parents and adult children are at risk of regressing into historic roles, treating each other and behaving as they did when the adult children were little kids.

In spite of its central importance to the quality of family relationships and business performance, most of us fail to appreciate how challenging communication can be. From my experience in working with family businesses, the challenge of effective communication is the illusion that we are good (if not great) communicators. Consequently, if there is a problem resulting from a miscommunication, we are prone to thinking it is the other person's fault.

We have a tendency to believe miscommunication is the fault of others and often don't hesitate to blame someone else. In fact, blaming someone else for miscommunication is as old as the Bible. Consider the following passage from the New Testament:

> Why do you see the speck that is in your brother's eye, but do not notice the log that is in your own eye? Or how can you say to your brother, "Let me take the speck out of your eye," when there is the log in your own eye? You hypocrite, first take the log out of your own eye, and then you will see clearly to take the speck out of your brother's eye.[1]

The material discussed in this chapter provides an introduction to the science behind why misunderstandings are so commonplace, making good communication difficult. Not appreciating our human foibles and believing we understand more than we actually do, we are prone to behaving arrogantly when dealing with others. Because the inherent challenges of human communication too often result in additional costs, lost revenue, lost opportunities, and strained and broken family relationships, imperfect communication is Failure Factor 3. This chapter explores this subject and offers some suggestions to improve the quality of communication within a family business, particularly by promoting the importance of humility.

The costs of communication breakdowns can be staggering. For example, if we assume that every employee mistake related to a failure in communication costs $10 per mistake, the assumed annual cost of communication breakdowns for a company with 50 employees would be $130,000 (i.e., $10 × 50 employees × 260 work days a year). However, many communication-related mistakes are even more costly than our hypothetical $10. The intangible costs resulting from interpersonal conflicts as a result of imperfect communication and misunderstandings can be far greater and much more problematic.

Swedish researchers recently reported that employees with leaders who were "inconsiderate, opaque, uncommunicative and poor advocates were approximately 60 percent more likely to suffer from a life threatening coronary condition than employees whose bosses exhibited positive leadership skills."[2]

Common Frustrations

Having witnessed many family conversations that ranged from merely unpleasant to downright explosive, I believe James Thurber could have been thinking about family businesses when he observed that "precision of communication is important, more important than ever, in our era of hair trigger balances, when a false or misunderstood word may create as much disaster as a sudden thought-less act." Simply consider the following expressions (or sentiments) I regularly hear when working with family businesses:

- "Another phony smile. Ugh."
- "That's not what we discussed."
- "He treats me like a child."
- "My opinion obviously doesn't count."

I have come to believe that such frustrations are often the unintended conse-quence of humans simply being poor communicators, not necessarily because they intend to be mean or dismissive. More specifically, I believe that in many cases a person responsible for appearing dismissive wasn't aware of actually being dismissive. Similarly, I believe that individuals who disagree on what was discussed often actually do have honestly different recollections about what was discussed.

> Dale Carnegie has observed that "when dealing with people, let us remember we are not dealing with creatures of logic. We are dealing with creatures of emotion, creatures bristling with prejudices and moti-vated by pride and vanity."[3]

Unfortunately, a variety of factors often conspire to keep great communica-tion from happening. As a result, in spite of having quantifiably more ways to communicate than at any time in human history, the quality of our communica-tion has ironically deteriorated.

Many great resources on communication provide valuable advice on how to improve virtually any type of relationship, such as:

1. Ask clarifying questions and repeat what has been heard to confirm that what was "heard" was actually "said."
2. Speak directly to another party whenever possible rather than delivering a message through a third party.
3. Speak honestly and candidly, yet politely and respectfully, about your feelings and perspectives.
4. Keep the lines of communication open and continuous, even if you dis-agree with someone on a position they take. Disagree agreeably.
5. Anticipate and proactively address issues in a constructive style. Recon-cile differing perspectives and opinions before decisions are made and before they become problems.
6. When angry, stop and count to ten before speaking.

Rather than simply recapitulating valuable advice on communication theory and strategy that is elsewhere widely available, this chapter continues to explore some fundamental insights into how we are hardwired through evolutionary adaptations to think and function—and (mis)communicate—as we do. As a result of our evolutionary adaptations, no single technique or combination of techniques offers family businesses more hope than creating and nurturing a culture of civility where family members and stakeholders are acculturated to work together and learn from each other, while being grounded in the humility that comes from realizing that we're not as perfect and infallible as we sometimes think we are.

Why We Sometimes Hear but Don't Listen

We have all heard the expression that simply because people can hear doesn't mean that they are also listening. When we hear, we tend to politely wait until another person is finished speaking and then share our thoughts and ideas. Sometimes, we are so impatient to share our thoughts that we interrupt the other person. In other instances, we may be in a conversation but distracted by something else that is competing for our attention.

Listening is more than literally hearing what others have to say; it involves trying to understand what others are saying. Listening can help us better understand how someone else sees and understands the world. The fact that we sometimes hear without listening can lead to problematic consequences in a family business when messages, directions, suggestions, and requests are unintentionally ignored because they were heard but not effectively processed.

In *Leadership by Example* Dr. Sanjiv Chopra explains:

> Leadership absolutely requires a respectful exchange of information, and that means listening as well as talking. The legendary corporate executive Lee Iacocca, who created some of the most successful models in automotive history while at Ford and transformed Chrysler, which was on the edge of bankruptcy, into an industry leader, once lamented, "I only wish I could find an institute that teaches people how to listen. Business people need to listen at least as much as they need to talk."[4]

Chopra notes that Yale Medical School and NYU Law School have gone so far as to hire actress and playwright Anna Deavere Smith to teach their students the art of listening.

While we might understandably get frustrated or disappointed with people who don't listen closely enough to what we are saying, rarely do we stop and think about the possibility that we might not be paying attention to them. Studies confirm that we believe we have listened and paid attention to others when, in reality, evidence suggests we haven't. In fact, some of these studies establish that our brains even process information in a variety of ways that can give us misplaced confidence in the accuracy of how our senses perceive the world.

In their fascinating book, *The Invisible Gorilla*, Professors Christopher Chabris and Daniel Simons describe a variety of experiments that demonstrate that our minds don't always work the way we think they do, resulting in the illusions that:

- we are paying attention when we aren't.
- our memories work like a camera, accurately recording details of events and experiences.
- we have well-founded confidence that "causes us to overestimate our own qualities, especially our abilities relative to other people."[5]
- we know more than we do by mistaking our knowledge of "what happens for an understanding of why it happens."[6]
- we see patterns in random acts and events, leading us to jump to conclusions by "[inferring] cause rather than coincidence."[7]
- our brains have "vast reservoirs of untapped mental ability . . . just waiting to be accessed."[8]

Each of these illusions about our mind's capacity and accuracy can create its own problematic communication issues in a family business. For example, consider what Chabris and Simon refer to as the "illusion of attention." Referring to studies that document the dangers of driving a car while talking on the phone, the authors note that "most people believe that as long as their eyes are on the road and their hands are on the wheel, they will see and react to any contingency." Extensive research, however, has documented that driving while talking on the phone is "comparable to the effects of driving while legally intoxicated."[9] Though we may believe our brains are comprehending a situation, they may be unable to do so with the accuracy we believe them capable of.

The human brain's ability to pay attention is physically constrained so that the more attention we pay to one matter, the less attention we are able to pay to anything else. The biology of our constrained mental resources helps explain why we are at risk of ignoring or misinterpreting what someone has to say to us. We might have heard but not listened.

The subject of hearing but not listening is complex and multifactorial. For example, one factor is the difference in communication styles between men and women. Deborah Tannen, one of the recognized experts in this field, notes that "[t]here *are* gender differences in ways of speaking, and we need to identify and understand them. Without such understanding, we are doomed to blame others or ourselves—or the relationship—for the otherwise mystifying and damaging effects of our contrasting conversational style."[10]

What This Means for Family Businesses

Studies like those reported by Chabris and Simon confirming we don't multitask well have great relevance to family businesses. Family conflict resulting from misunderstandings due to divided attention happens with unfortunate regularity, as seen through the Adidas/Puma split discussed in chapter 1. Family businesses might consider adopting a few basic rules designed to improve the attention paid to communication, such as a rule prohibiting the use of cell phones, laptops, and other technologies in any meeting, or a rule directing people not to send or respond to e-mails while on the phone. Such rules would help improve the quality of attention paid to a message, reducing the likelihood of "hearing but not listening." Such rules would also enhance the quality of nonverbal communication between individuals, reinforcing the bonds of trust that result from more focused and intentional communication.

The Science of Nonverbal Communication

Whether conscious of it or not, we are all experts at interpreting signals—the nonverbal cues we communicate through a variety of means, including gestures, body language, facial expressions, the pitch and volume of voice, and the presence or absence of eye contact. Think of an occasion in which you were speaking with someone who never looked you in the eyes and, perhaps, even continued to multitask, focusing on another project while only partially listening to you. Then think of another occasion in which that person dropped what he or she was doing and, looking directly into your eyes, concentrated on what you had to say. Even if the words spoken in both conversations were identical, most of us would find the quality of the latter conversation to be much more satisfying than the quality of the former. Such is the power of nonverbal communication.

Modern technology has enabled the creation of social media sites that allow family members and countless "friends" to share photos, personal updates, and messages with each other. Sherry Turkle, a professor in the Program of Science, Technology, and Society at MIT, has observed that "we are tempted to think that our little 'sips' of online connection add up to a big gulp of real conversation. But they don't. E-mail, Twitter,

(continued)

Facebook, all of these have their places—in politics, commerce, romance and friendship. But no matter how valuable, they do not substitute for conversation."[11] Families need to set aside time to get together to talk, to enjoy each other's company, and to work on their family business.

One of the early pioneers in the study of nonverbal communication was Professor Albert Mehrabian, who, along with Susan Ferris, published a study in 1967 that described the relative importance of words, tone of voice, and body language in communication. In one of the experiments, subjects listened to nine recorded words, spoken with different tones of voice, three of which were intended to convey "liking" ("honey," "dear," and "thanks"), three of which were intended to convey "neutrality" ("maybe," "really," and "oh"), and three of which were intended to convey "disliking" ("don't," "brute," and "terrible"). The subjects were asked to guess the emotions behind the spoken words. Finding that "tone of voice" was more important than the actual words used, Mehrabian and his colleagues proposed the following widely quoted statistics on communication dynamics that, whether specifically or "directionally" accurate, are important to consider:

- 7 percent of our feelings and attitudes are attributable to the actual words that are spoken.
- 38 percent of our feelings and attitudes are attributable to how the words are spoken, including tone of voice.
- 55 percent of our feelings and attitudes are attributable to body language, including facial expressions and gestures.[12]

Professor Alex Pentland, director of the Human Dynamics Laboratory at MIT, is a leading authority on our ability to communicate by reading each other's nonverbal signals, such as gestures and facial expressions. Pentland explains that "a relative newcomer in hominid evolution, language was likely layered upon older primate signaling mechanisms that used social network strategies to find resources, make decisions and coordinate group action."[13] Work by Pentland and others explains why "what we say" is often less important than "how we say it," because, for example, of our ability to send and receive messages through:

- body language (e.g., gestures, eye contact, nodding, smiling, frowning);
- emotion (e.g., inflection, tone of voice, such as criticism, sarcasm, sincerity); and
- other nonverbal connections and signals (e.g., whether the people communicating are friends or enemies, and whether they share similarities or differences, such as age, education, religion, and experience).

Professor Pentland and his team at MIT have determined that nonverbal signals not only are very reliably processed but also can trigger physiological changes in people receiving the signals. For instance, signals that might once have increased the energy level within a hunting team can be used to increase the energy level in a business team through "contagious excitement." This research also demonstrates how these signals can be used to create cohesion by increasing empathy and trust through mimicking the signals of other family members.[14]

> Leo Tolstoy magnificently captures the power of nonverbal communication with this exchange from *Anna Karenina*:
>
> > Levin listened and thought and could not think of anything to say. Nikolay probably felt the same. He began asking his brother about his affairs, and Levin was glad to talk about himself, because then he could talk without pretending. He told his brother his plans and activities.
> >
> > His brother listened but obviously was not interested.
> >
> > These two men were so dear and close to each other that the slightest movement, the tone of the voice, told both more than it was possible to say in words.[15]

What This Means for Family Businesses

Communication happens in ways other than simply through the use of words. As a result, stakeholders in family businesses are well served by learning to appreciate that the most reliable way to communicate is face-to-face, and to use facial and other expressions that communicate interest, understanding, and other positive emotions as often as possible. Whether intentionally or unintentionally, our nonverbal signals can provoke negative emotions and responses or can generate energy, enthusiasm, collegiality, and other positive emotions. Family businesses might find individuals more productive, more creative, and more satisfied simply as a result of having been given the opportunity to engage in open, robust, engaging, and constructive conversations.

While less personal forms of communication such as e-mails and telephone calls can't realistically be abandoned, family business stakeholders should be mindful of the challenges of communicating information in these ways. Since so many of the issues in family businesses can be emotional, efforts should be made to increase face-to-face meetings on any subject that is potentially sensitive.

How Our Imperfect Memories Can Create Communication Problems

Since Benjamin Franklin's observation that "creditors have better memories than debtors," scientists have learned a great deal about human memories.

The more we learn, the more imperfect we realize our memories are and how that can create another type of communication problem within a family business.

Think of an important event in your life—your marriage, the birth of your child, your graduation from school. Can you remember what you were wearing? How you dressed and what you ate that day? How many similar details can you recall from the day before or the day after those major events? I suspect very few. Have you ever forgotten where you left your car keys? Or parked your car? Thought experiments like these help us to appreciate that our memories don't work like video cameras, accurately storing our every experience in perfect detail. In *The Seven Sins of Memory*, Daniel Schacter, chairman of Harvard's psychology department, proposes that memory's malfunctions can be divided into the following seven fundamental "transgressions" or "sins":

1. **Transience**, which refers to memory's "use-it-or-lose-it" quality. When we recall an event, we are actually recalling a reconstruction of the actual event, and how we reconstruct an event changes over time. As a result, the details of what actually happened become fuzzy as the memories of one experience blur with similar experiences, making it hard to distinguish what actually happened.[16]

2. **Absentmindedness**, which refers to the failure to pay enough attention to an event to properly encode it in our memory. For example, we may forget where we placed a pen because we were thinking of something else at the time. Dividing our attention "reduces the overall amount of cognitive resources—the 'energy supply' that fuels encoding—that can be devoted to incoming information."[17]

3. **Blocking**, which refers to the inability to easily retrieve information that remains stored in our memory, such as when information is "on the tip of your tongue."

4. **Misattribution**, which refers to when the components associated with one event are recalled as part of our recollection of another event, creating confusion about what we experienced and what we imagine.[18]

5. **Suggestibility**, which refers to the "tendency to incorporate misleading information from external sources—other people, written materials or pictures, even the media—into personal recollections," leading us to think that what has been suggested is a real memory.[19]

6. **Bias**, which refers to how our experiences, beliefs, knowledge, and mood filter our perceptions and experiences and how they are encoded in our memories.

7. **Persistence**, which refers to memories that are hard to forget, usually because they are recollections associated with traumatic events. However, even some of these memories may become distorted over time.[20]

When we experience an event or acquire a new fact, complex chemical changes occur at the brain's junctions that connect neurons with one another. Experiments indicate that with the passage of time, these connections can weaken and disappear, eventually making recall impossible.[21]

Many interesting experiments have demonstrated various aspects of how our memories fail us. For example, it seems that the average person will remember only about one-half to one-third of what was said after only a few hours, and only about 25 percent of what was said after two hours.[22] As a thought experiment, consider the last conversation you had. Take out a pencil and pad of paper and write as much of that conversation as you can recall, word for word. I'm confident that you'll be able to recall the gist of the discussion but I suspect that most readers will be unable to accurately recall the specific words used.

Our imperfect memories can create a myriad of problems. For example, since we can't read others' minds, we might be unable to distinguish between when someone honestly can't recall a promise made and when we have been intentionally lied to. Perhaps relying too much on our ancestral brain's instinctual or emotional response, we might think that we are being lied to on purpose, and that the party lying to us is doing so to serve his or her personal agenda. As a result, numerous family feuds have begun with the innocent and unintentional failure of memory.

Professor Gary Marcus notes that a kindred problem to having imperfect memories is that the source of our memories can be equally poor. He writes that:

> For our ancestors, who lived almost entirely in the here and now (as virtually all nonhuman life forms still do), quick access to contextually relevant memories of recent events or frequently occurring ones helped navigate the challenges of seeking food or avoiding danger. . . Concerns about misattribution or bias in courtroom testimony simply don't apply.[23]

What This Means for Family Businesses

The fact that our memories are imperfect has important implications for every family business. There are, of course, countless resources available that can help improve our memories through techniques such as the use of visual imagery or mnemonics. These techniques can be quite helpful, but they have their limits. Even if we could find a way for everyone to learn one of these memory-enhancing methods, our brains are still incapable of remembering every detail of every conversation.

While "handshake understandings" are great, family businesses would be well served by recognizing the importance of managing our imperfect memories, and summarizing particularly important conversations in writing. Notes or minutes should be taken to record major decisions made at meetings, and important agreements should be documented and maintained in a safe place.

We Are Prone to Exaggerate and Lie

While I suspect that most of us generally regard honesty as a universal virtue, it seems nearly as true that we are all, even to some minor degree, dishonest. Examples might be "a little white lie," like saying someone looks good when you don't really think so, or stating that you are doing well when you're feeling somewhat depressed. As it turns out, honesty and lying are much more complicated concepts than we typically realize. Unfortunately, our propensity to exaggerate or lie can add up over time and breed mistrust within a family business.

> *"The least initial deviation from the truth is multiplied later a thousand fold."*
>
> Aristotle

Dan Ariely, the James B. Duke Professor of Psychology at Duke University, published a book titled *The (Honest) Truth About Dishonesty: How We Lie to Everyone—Especially Ourselves.* This book continues to add to our body of knowledge about how and why we think and act as we do. Professor Ariely discusses how we all essentially cheat "up to the level that allows us to retain our self-image as reasonably honest individuals."[24] More specifically, Ariely proposes that:

> On the one hand, we want to view ourselves as honest, honorable people. We want to be able to look at ourselves in the mirror and feel good about ourselves . . . On the other hand, we want to benefit from cheating and get as much money as possible.[25]

This is where our amazing cognitive flexibility comes into play. As long as we cheat by only a little bit, we can benefit from cheating and still view ourselves as marvelous human beings. This balancing act is a form of rationalization.[26]

What This Means for Family Businesses

The fact that most of us lie in one fashion or another can have important implications for family businesses. While we might consider acts of dishonesty to be petty and insignificant, they can have massive ramifications. Frederick Nietzsche once proclaimed, "I'm not upset that you lied to me, I'm upset that from now on I can't believe you." Once one loses confidence in another's regard for truth, everything is exposed to doubt and, little by little, relationships are prone to deteriorate and break down. Because a family business depends on family members trusting each other, the erosion of integrity and trust can create significant problems—perhaps particularly so if, as Daniel Ariely's research confirms, when people feel like "everybody's doing it," they are more likely to lie and cheat too.[27] And so a pernicious downward spiral is born.

While there may be no single magic bullet to prevent people from lying, certain mechanisms and attitudes can help. Family businesses should purposefully and explicitly emphasize the importance of honesty as a virtue. Leaders should model honesty and offenders should be warned that dishonesty isn't tolerated. Ground rules should be discussed and published addressing the consequences for repeated instances of lying.

This is not to advocate a rigid adherence to telling the literal truth at all times and in all circumstances, which can often be insensitive or mean. Sometimes, the challenge in striving for constructive communication is that relationships might be best served by a "little white lie." Family businesses are happier places to work when family members strike a sometimes difficult—but critical—balance. Striking this delicate balance starts with appreciating the problem. In my life, I have found it helpful to be as rigidly honest as possible and tell a "little white lie" only if two factors are met: first, it is distinctly "little," and, second, more importantly, it is told to benefit or protect someone else.

We Like to Hear Ourselves Talk

We can all think of people who, having mastered the art of talking, seem to have failed to master the art of listening. As it turns out, this is another aspect of our brains' hardwiring. In a recent study at Harvard University, neuroscientist Diana Tamir and her colleagues discovered that the gratification we receive when we share our thoughts and ideas with others actually creates a response in our brains that is similar to the response created when we enjoy food or sex. Tamir's study revealed that "people were even willing to forgo money in order to talk about themselves."[28]

> We are often admonished that we have two ears and one mouth so that we can listen twice as much as we speak.

In their book, *The New Art of Managing People*, Phillip L. Hunsaker and Anthony J. Alessandra discuss their findings about listening, learning, communicating, and their impact on working with people. There are many different learning and listening styles, including:

- **The Non-Listener**, who does not make any effort to listen, does most of the talking, interrupts, does not let anyone else get a word in, and must be the last to speak.
- **The Marginal Listener**, who may nod and feign interest, but is listening only at a superficial level, resulting in frequent misunderstandings.
- **The Evaluative Listener**, who hears what is being said without fully understanding the message, often resulting in misconstruing the speaker's real intent or message.
- **The Active Listener**, who listens carefully, not only through hearing, but also by paying attention to body language, voice inflections, and other nonverbal signals; and who tries to appreciate the other person's perspective, asks questions, and listens carefully to the answers.

Hunsaker and Alessandra note that:

Ineffective listening is one of the most frequent causes of misunderstandings, mistakes, jobs that need to be redone, and lost sales and customers . . . Poor listening is a factor in low employee morale and increased turnover because employees do not feel their managers listen to their needs, suggestions, or complaints.[29]

What This Means for Family Businesses

There are many great resources on how to be a better listener. However, I have not yet seen advice on how to talk less. Family businesses would be wise to apply some of the most basic suggestions offered by communication experts, including formally or informally making sure everyone at a meeting has an appropriate opportunity to speak, to be heard, and to ask questions. Families who work to create an environment where individuals feel like they can share their opinions and ideas are more likely to feel good about their business and build rewarding relationships. Families might also consider coaching family members to avoid interrupting someone speaking and to avoid the urge to get their point in. With some practice, family members will learn to speak less and listen more.

Humility and Communication (Success Factor 3)

Leadership experts and executive coaches often identify humility as a critical attribute to being a successful leader. John Baldoni, an author and authority on leadership, explains that "[a] sense of humility is essential to leadership because it authenticates a person's humanity. We humans are frail creatures; we have our faults. Recognizing what we do well, as well as what we do not do so well, is vital to self-awareness and paramount to humility."[30]

Baldoni offers the following suggestions on how humility in the workplace can be demonstrated:

Temper authority. Power comes with rank but you don't have to pull it to make it work for you. You can encourage others to make decisions by delegating authority and responsibility. Encourage your people to write their own performance objectives and set team goals. Allow them to make decisions. Your authority comes in the form of imposing order and discipline.

Look to promote others. . . . a characteristic of successful managers is their ability to promote others, sometimes to positions higher than their own. Such managers are talent groomers, they are the ones upon whose leadership success of the enterprise rests.

Acknowledge what others do. Few have said it better than legendary Alabama coach Paul "Bear" Bryant. "If anything goes bad, I did it. If anything goes semi-good, we did it. If anything goes really good, then you did it. That's all it takes to get people to win football games for you." Practice that attitude always, especially when things are not going well, and your team will rally together because they want you to succeed. In short, humility breeds humility.[31]

As scientists have found creative ways to calculate and measure the impact of humility on performance within organizations and teams, it has become demonstrably clear that religion and philosophy have been right all along in promoting the importance of humility. For example, Professor Bradley Owens at the University of Buffalo School of Management and his colleagues note that:

leaders' display of humility has positive motivational effects on the employees they lead. . . . [W]hen leaders show what may be viewed as a lack of humility (taking all the credit for success, over estimating their contributions relative to others, not listening) followers disengage and lose their motivation to work hard under their leader.[32]

The body of knowledge on humility suggests that humble leaders are not only better liked than arrogant leaders but are more effective as well. Professor Owens explains that "growing and learning often involves failure and can be embarrassing" but that "leaders who can overcome their fears and broadcast their feelings as they work through the messy internal growth process will be viewed more favorably by their followers. They also will legitimize their followers' own growth journeys and will have higher-performing organizations."[33]

Humility is an off-cited core value in many leading family businesses. For example, Jimmy Haslam III, the CEO of Pilot Flying J., a family business that operates gas stations and truck stops, indicated that one of the most important pieces of advice that his father shared with him was to "be humble and ask a lot of questions."[34]

> Families would be well served by "teaching humility," including, for example, the following strategies:
>
> 1. Help individuals to appreciate their talents while understanding their limitations.
> 2. Help individuals to not simply judge others and their faults but also to recognize their own faults.
> 3. Encourage family members to stop comparing themselves to others.
> 4. Focus on understanding and appreciating the talents, experiences, and contributions of others.
> 5. Help others to understand that mistakes are expected and not to be afraid to admit to having made a mistake. Encourage learning from mistakes so that, in time, they are understood as lessons.
> 6. Think about blessings and good fortune. Family members should be reminded that much of their current success is due to the foundation laid by others who came before them.
> 7. Explicitly discuss humility.

Humility's particular relevance to a discussion about communication is due to the fact that our brains process information in ways that can easily derail constructive conversations. We often fail to recognize our role in creating a communication problem, tending, instead, to assign blame to another person who (we think) isn't smart or sensitive enough to understand the real issues, facts, challenges, or opportunities.

> One of the world's longest continuously operating family businesses was Kongo Gumi, a Japanese temple builder that operated under the founders' descendants from 578 to 2006, when it succumbed to excess debt and an

unfavorable business climate. One of the factors credited with this family business's success was the practice (common in Japan) of sons-in-law taking the family name when they joined the family firm.[35] This allowed the company to continue under the same name, even when there were no sons in a given generation. While I'm not endorsing that as a planning strategy for family businesses, I do think it speaks to the importance of humility in a family business, in this case the humility of sons-in-law who chose to put the interest of their family business before their sense of personal identity.

Rabbi John A. Linder, before becoming the Senior Rabbi of Temple Solel in Phoenix, Arizona, was an executive at United Alloys & Steel, his family's successful scrap steel business in Buffalo, New York. Observing that there is no more treasured virtue in Judaism than humility, Rabbi Linder emphasizes that the more one accomplishes, the more humility weighs as a counterbalance. He notes that there is a Jewish custom to carry two notes in your pockets at all times. One reads, "The world was created for my sake"—reminding us that each person has unique gifts and an obligation to use them for good in the world. The other note reads, "I am but dust and ashes"—reminding us to not get too carried away with ourselves. Humility, Rabbi Linder teaches us, is the space between the two.

Conclusion

I believe that one of the ways science can benefit any family business is by helping to sensitize its stakeholders to the value of humility, particularly as we learn that:

1. Our judgment is distorted and the quality of our decisions impaired because we routinely "hear" but don't "listen";
2. Our memories are imperfect and often unreliable;
3. We are prone to exaggerate and lie;
4. We prefer to talk rather than listen; and
5. While we pay more attention to nonverbal signals than to the words that are used, we don't always stop and appreciate the fact that others are paying attention to our nonverbal signals. These can inadvertently distract someone from the real message we are seeking to share.

I offer three suggestions to improve communication among families in business together:

First, families should incorporate a variety of traditional strategies as part of an overall program to improve communication and enhance the likelihood of people understanding each other as much as possible, including by:

1. Encouraging questioning to verify understanding;
2. Encouraging careful attention not just to words but to nonverbal signals;
3. Encouraging sensitivity to the importance of tone of voice so that the meaning of words is enhanced by positive feelings and emotions;
4. Encouraging awareness of body language so that positive and negative messages are appropriately and thoughtfully sent;
5. Keeping an open-door policy that encourages robust conversation where issues can be shared, processed, understood, and addressed without fear of recrimination;
6. Addressing concerns before they become problems; and
7. Acknowledging the value of others by complimenting their behavior.

Second, families in business together would also be well served by ensuring that meetings are thoughtfully designed to promote constructive conversations. Some helpful suggestions include:

1. Setting a clear agenda that ensures focus and limits rambling.
2. Imposing a "no devices" rule so that attention isn't diverted by e-mails, texts, and phone calls.
3. Ensuring that everyone participates in some fashion.
4. Limiting the time people might speak on a point to avoid monopolization of a discussion.
5. Setting an end time for the meeting and sticking to it so individuals can plan their schedules and not be worried by other commitments if a meeting runs late.
6. Encouraging the expression of honest differences to get the benefit of everyone's best ideas.
7. Holding regularly scheduled meetings to ensure that stakeholders are well informed.

Finally, for a variety of reasons, our human nature makes it impossible to communicate perfectly. Our tendency to make faulty assumptions, to "hear but not listen," and to behave or process information in a variety of imperfect ways creates problems. Perhaps the most significant problem is our tendency to think that if there is a communication problem, it is someone else's fault because we are pretty good communicators. Consequently, perhaps the most important, yet infrequently discussed, strategy is to intentionally and explicitly adopt an attitude of humility as the most effective way to enhance our self-awareness of our role in miscommunications.

The impact of Success Factor 3—humility—is reflected in Figure 9.

Figure 9: The Impact of Success Factor 3—Humility

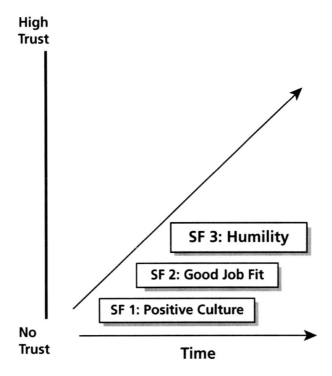

However hard we try to communicate constructively, we'll continue to make unintended blunders and mistakes. Because I believe that family businesses fail more from such blunders than from purposefully evil deeds, "structural safety nets" need to be put in place to minimize the likelihood (and consequences) of such blunders. Some of the most essential safety nets are explored in the following chapters.

Quotations

"The single biggest problem in communication is the illusion that it has taken place."

George Bernard Shaw

"The greatest thing in family life is to take a hint when a hint is intended—and not to take a hint when a hint isn't intended."

Robert Frost

"I like to listen. I have learned a great deal from listening carefully. Most people never listen."

Ernest Hemingway

"In the whole round of human affairs little is so fatal to peace as misunderstanding."

Margaret Elizabeth Sangster

"It is singular how soon we lose the impression of what ceases to be constantly before us. A year impairs, a luster obliterates. There is little distinct left without an effort of memory, then indeed the lights are rekindled for a moment—but who can be sure that the Imagination is not the torch-bearer?"

Lord Byron

"A conversation is a dialogue, not a monologue. That's why there are so few good conversations: due to scarcity, two intelligent talkers seldom meet."

Truman Capote

"Pretty much all the honest truth telling in the world is done by children."

Oliver Wendell Holmes

"Men occasionally stumble over the truth, but most of them pick themselves up and hurry off as if nothing had happened."

Winston Churchill

"Whoever is careless with the truth in small matters cannot be trusted with important matters."

Albert Einstein

"Once we realize that imperfect understanding is the human condition there is no shame in being wrong, only in failing to correct our mistakes."

George Soros

"If I have seen further than others, it is because I have stood on the shoulders of giants."

Sir Isaac Newton

"Humility is the foundation of all the other virtues hence, in the soul in which this virtue does not exist there cannot be any other virtue except in mere appearance."

Saint Augustine

An Introduction to P/E Max 6

"We've learned . . . that the soft stuff and the hard stuff are becoming increasingly intertwined. A company's values—what it stands for, what its people believe in—are crucial to its competitive success. Indeed, values drive the business."[1]

Robert Haas, former chairman and CEO, Levi Strauss

Background: Failure Factor 4 (Unprincipled Decision Making)

The material in the previous chapters highlights the enormous benefit family businesses can realize from the effort to create a healthy and positive culture by emphasizing civility, appreciation, and humility, as well as by promoting the happiness of individual family members by helping them find their life callings. Such efforts can easily and painlessly result in improved, if not beautifully coordinated and noncontroversial, operations within a family.

However, "beautifully coordinated" shouldn't imply "perfectly coordinated." Most human beings aren't saints and, as the prior chapters pointed out, they certainly don't function and process information with the precision and accuracy of computers. The natural result of our human susceptibility to making mistakes in judgment is particularly problematic in family businesses. Family businesses are inherently complex organizations made up of individuals who have their own singular perspectives on life and what is good for the family business that are influenced by unique natures, environments, and "life circumstances" (such as health, marriage, divorce, children, finances, etc.). The combination of those individual perspectives with natural, fear-based instincts and accompanying negative emotions can easily get in the way of smooth coordination in spite of the antidotes to failure suggested in the previous chapters. These consequences can be experienced as ranging from occasional, benign difficulties in securing stakeholder consensus to outright family conflict.

Failure Factor 4 describes the divisive decision-making environment in which families make ad hoc decisions while failing to account for their individual members' unique perspectives, often resulting in heated emotional reactions when people feel they are being treated unfairly.

> A chaotic decision-making environment can help explain the challenges parents experience when seeking to make decisions, the results of which might be different depending on whether they consider the matter as "owner" or "parent." The failure to constructively reconcile these sometimes differing perspectives can result in a parent making inconsistent decisions over time, creating and exacerbating tension and conflict in a family business.

The antidote to Failure Factor 4 is the thoughtful articulation of unifying and mediating core principles, including a statement of core values, a mission statement, a vision statement, and appropriate policies—particularly when applied on a foundation constructed of the first three success factors (positive culture, intelligent fit, and humble communication). As many organizations have already discovered, the articulation of guiding core principles and a commitment to them (a culture I refer to as "P/E Max" for reasons discussed below) can significantly help family business stakeholders more rationally and peacefully reconcile their divergent individual perspectives and, in the process, help maintain a nice coordination of efforts.

> Imperfect thinking, including faulty memories, hearing but not listening, and reacting in "fear mode," represents a major challenge to any family business that requires a variety of safeguards and antidotes. Chapter 7 will explain how family businesses can benefit from establishing a strong board of directors. That discussion complements the material in this chapter by explaining how family members in business together can make better decisions.

A Family without a Compass

Because people are inherently unique, it is not surprising that family members might regularly disagree on whether a particular decision is good or bad. Ideally, the existence of divergent perspectives can lead, through constructive conversations, to more considered and better decisions. We are all familiar with the proverb that "two heads are better than one." I have found, however, that holding and advocating divergent or contrarian views in a family business that operates without a "decision-making compass" (particularly where the culture is predominately negative and fear-based) tends to lead to random, dysfunctional, divisive—and ultimately destructive—decisions.

Some years ago, I was retained by a large industrial family business in the Midwest that was being managed by a widow, her eldest son, and several siblings who sat on the company's board of directors. The agenda for our first meeting included a discussion on the merits of expanding operations into the South, even though the family had already spent more than $25 million toward the construction of a new facility for that purpose. The siblings had yet to agree on whether expansion was a good or a bad decision. After facilitating several long and difficult family meetings designed to sharpen the family's thoughts on strategy and interests, they decided to pull the plug and sell their uncompleted facility at a substantial loss. That decision was not only costly but it severely strained family relationships.

A family business's early success can make consensus increasingly difficult to reach as new family members join the business, diminishing the chances for long-term success over the generations. As the business succeeds, the number of family members who own and work in the business ordinarily increases as the founder (or cofounders) have children and grandchildren who might, as stakeholders, be interested in the business, as a result of inheriting an ownership interest, working in the business (or having a spouse working in the business), or both. This changing decision-making dynamic is reflected in Figure 10. The incremental increase in the number of family members interested in the enterprise simultaneously increases the number of individuals who might naturally be more attentive to ongoing business decisions. The greater number of participants considering the merits of decisions increases the odds of disagreement.

Figure 10: The Calculus of Decision Dynamics

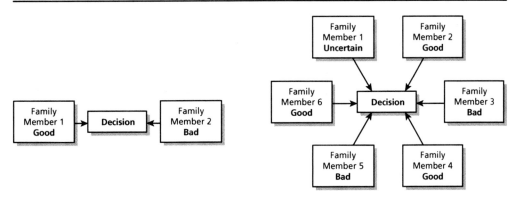

In *Born to Rebel*, Frank Sulloway, an MIT-based scholar applying evolutionary theory to family dynamics, persuasively articulates a theory about the link between latter-born children and creativity. Recognizing that "siblings raised together are almost as different in their personalities as people from different families," he offers as an explanation that many such differences are a result of siblings adopting different strategies to secure parental favor. Considering the subject of birth order from a Darwinian perspective, Sulloway highlights why firstborns tend to identify with authority while latter-born siblings increasingly tend to challenge the status quo, occasionally to the point of rebelling, explaining:

> Siblings become different for the same reason that species do over time: divergence minimizes competition for scarce resources. For example, children can increase the amount of nurturing and attention they receive from parents if they avoid direct competition and instead appeal to whichever parent is unencumbered. The story of sibling differences is the story of family structure and how niches are partitioned within it. It is also the story of parental investment and any perceived biases in it.[2]

Sulloway's compelling theory may help explain why family members can have widely divergent views on the merits of their business decisions. It might also help explain why passively interested family members can sometimes feel that their siblings who are actively involved in the business are "favored" by the additional parental time and attention that results from working together.

As different as siblings might be, the differences between cousins are typically even greater. James "Jay" Hughes Jr., a lawyer, author, and prominent authority on family businesses, writes:

> One of the difficulties for families trying to govern themselves is that members tend to think of themselves mainly in vertical relations to one another. Each member measures his place in the family in relation to parents, grandparents, and great-grandparents. Family members rarely view themselves horizontally, in relation to siblings and cousins. Yet it is each generation, horizontally, that bears the critical duty of renewing the family's social compact if a family is to preserve its wealth over the long term.[3]

Individual family members can also struggle to balance their personal and professional perspectives on business decisions as a result of not having thought through how to best reconcile conflicting family and business values, such as those highlighted in Figure 1 in chapter 1.

Family business authorities Grant Gordon and Nigel Nicholson, describing a recipe for family business success, observe that

> [b]rothers can work together wonderfully well ... there are good genetic reasons for siblings to stick together. They have more interests in common than either of them has with outsiders. But the dynamic of siblings is that they come into conflict when they are locked into a single space, sharing resources to get to the same goal—there can only be one top dog. If they are able to differentiate themselves and find their own space it is easier.[4]

Family Values Can Differ from Business Values

The inevitability that family members will have differing opinions, and that individuals will find themselves conflicted about the merits of certain decisions, results from the fact that one's interests and values as a family member might stand in stark contrast to the interests and values that might be held when considering the business perspective.

Consider, for example, a parent who provides a child with a position in the family business so that he or she might have a lucrative income and a prestigious position—notwithstanding the fact that the child is incapable of discharging his or her responsibilities effectively because of a poor fit with actual skill and talents. For many parents, the decision would make total sense, as evolution has hardwired parents to promote offspring survival, growth, and development.[5] However, that parent might have some angst employing the child when considering the decision from the perspective of a business owner. The failure to reconcile one's roles and responsibilities as a parent with those as a business owner can easily lead to the family business paying a stiff financial price, and, in turn, to family conflict as other family members get frustrated by inconsistent and self-serving decisions.

One example of a family business that suffered financially from failing to more carefully work through these issues is the Bronfman family, well known for the massive fortune built from owning Seagram's and substantial stakes in Conoco Oil and DuPont chemicals. Gordon and Nicholson report that the family experienced a substantial decline in its fortune after 31-year-old Edgar Bronfman Jr. took control of the company and sold Seagram's to Vivendi, a French media and entertainment conglomerate, in exchange for Vivendi's shares, which plummeted soon after the deal was consummated. Commenting on this family business debacle, they write:

The decision to appoint a person without obvious experience other than a career in show business, which appeared to be going nowhere fast, to a post of such high responsibility says more about the father than the son. Handing his son of 31 years the baton of leadership could be seen as Edgar Sr's riposte to his late father, who he felt had not loved him and had hung on to power at the firm too late in life. This was a demonstrable act of faith in his son, a boy in whom he could see no faults. It would prove to be an act of serious misjudgment and a near-fatal blow to the business and its shareholders.[6]

Without a smart approach to managing these divergent family and business value systems, decisions inside family businesses are at risk of being made inconsistently and arbitrarily, sometimes from a family perspective and sometimes from a business perspective. The resulting ad hoc decision-making culture can be problematic among siblings and, perhaps, even more so in a third- or later-generation business populated by cousins who sense that decisions are biased, typically, for example, in support of "family" when the decision maker's children are involved—but biased toward "business" when involving the decision maker's nieces and nephews.

An Introduction to P/E Max

The chaotic and destructive decision-making environment characterized by Failure Factor 4 is a natural consequence of individuals coming together, often initially with genuine love for each other and a commitment to the family business. However, possessing the human foibles highlighted in earlier chapters and lacking clarity about how best to pursue their individual and collective goals, family members are prone to making inconsistent "gut decisions." Individuals will have differing perspectives and interests on issues over time that can be easily misunderstood as self-serving, adding to the erosion of trust and diminishing the likelihood of success in a family business. For reasons that become apparent below, I describe them as "expedient decisions."

I have found that the antidote to this fourth failure factor is to develop a decision-making environment that is the antithesis of an expedient environment, one in which clear and appropriate policies are used consistently. I describe these as "principled decisions" to reflect the fact that behavior is consistent with one's principles, and I have found that the base formula for effective decision making is a function of a new (nonfinancial) "P/E ratio": the ratio of principle-based decisions to expedient decisions. The goal of this decision-making model is to help families function entirely in the numerator, making only principled decisions, a metric I refer to as "P/E Max." By contrast, I refer to expedient decisions and actions that are inconsistent with core principles as "P/E Low."

In my early work with family businesses, I confess to having struggled to find any benefit to developing a mission statement, a vision statement, and a statement of core values. Too often, I'd find myself in the lobby of a company that had its core principles hanging in a fancy frame, only to discover that those principles held little more than decorative significance. Over the years, I have come to appreciate that one of the most important steps a family business (or any organization) can take is to develop its core values and authentically integrate them into its culture. Jay Hughes Jr. captures the importance of principled decision making in a family business when he notes:

> Because a family is, by definition, two or more individuals, any decision made by a family must involve joint decision making. Joint decision making expresses a system of governance. . . .

> When a family recognizes that its decision making process is a form of governance, it also intuitively understands that by organizing itself to make joint decisions instead of individual and ad hoc decisions, it has a better chance of making good decisions than bad.[7]

The remainder of this chapter explores how family businesses can become high-performance organizations by creating and implementing the key components of "principle-based decisions"—a statement of core values, a mission statement, a vision statement, and key policies—and how these tools can be used as a compass to help guide decisions and create alignment within the family business.

> Aside from helping create strong alignment around a family business's organizational goals and objectives, studies suggest that individual well-being is enhanced when values are congruent with social environment.[8]

A Statement of Values

Jeffrey Abrahams collected more than 300 mission statements from some of the largest companies in the United States, writing that "[v]alues are the collective principles and ideals which guide the thoughts and actions of an individual, or a group of individuals."[9] Authentically held values that are used in a consistent fashion can align behavior, functioning like a decision-making compass, helping to promote integrity, collaboration, and high trust among members of a team.

Because of their role in aligning positive and productive actions, the most successful companies empower employees by encouraging day-to-day behavior that is consistent with organizational values. In *Built to Last*, Jim Collins and Jerry

Porras observe that "[c]ontrary to business school doctrine, we did not find 'max-imizing shareholder wealth' . . . as the dominant driving force or primary objec-tive through the history of most visionary companies . . . [Rather,] they had a core ideology to a greater degree than the comparison companies in our study."[10] Great companies, rather than getting bogged down in micromanaging employ-ees, empower their employees through authentically shared values that reflect a philosophy toward doing business in a smart and collaborative manner. In value-driven organizations, if a decision or action is consistent with reasoned, articu-lated values, it is right. Insight from the science of positive psychology suggests that family businesses are well served by creating a statement of core values to help ensure consistent and unbiased decisions and actions that both enhance the likelihood of success and ensure that family members are treated fairly.

Scientific Insights on the Importance of Values

The scientific study of values offers important insights and suggests numerous applications for family businesses and their advisers. For example:

1. Chris Peterson, one of the founding fathers of positive psychology, observes that "[t]here is a theoretical possibility of individuals or groups that function well without values. But they seem not to exist."[11] Peterson observes that "[s]hared values regularize behavior within a group in an efficient way by articulating a general rule that applies broadly, so group members are spared the ongoing reinvention of standards and justifications."[12] If they haven't yet prepared a statement of values, family businesses might take no better next step than to do so to help ensure smoother functioning.

2. Research also confirms that people are happier when they know their values and live in alignment with them.[13] Value-driven family businesses not only offer the potential for economic returns and commercial oppor-tunities to family members, they also promote a supportive, nurturing environment that enhances quality of life.

3. Chris Peterson and Martin Seligman developed the Values in Action Inventory of Strengths (VIA-IS), a psychological assessment that, by pos-ing a series of questions, ranks an individual's strengths from 1 to 24. The top five strengths are considered "signature strengths."[14] Peterson and Seligman suggest that the VIA-IS could be used to help people capi-talize and build upon their signature strengths, rather than the more tra-ditional approach of identifying "lesser strengths" (or weaknesses) and helping people improve those.[15] The VIA-IS survey is available online at www.viacharacter.org.

These and other scientific findings suggest that family businesses are well served by identifying, articulating, and promoting value-based behavior.

Examples of Value Statements

Generally speaking, no business value is "better" or "worse," or "right" or "wrong." The only requirement is that the articulated values authentically represent what is most important to a particular organization. The statement is typically limited to core values to distinguish those that are merely relevant from those that are deeply held. Some examples of values frequently used by organizations include: collaborative, committed, dependable, disciplined, flexible, friendly, honest, innovative, passionate, and positive.

There is no particular form the value statement should follow nor is there a single right way to describe organizational values. Some companies might simply refer to their "values," others to their "core values," and others to "what we believe in." Consider the following examples from a few of the largest and most respected family businesses in the world.

Mars, Inc. (a $30-billion-a-year business known for a variety of products, including chocolate, Wrigley's gum, and Uncle Ben's rice):

The Five Principles of Mars:

1. Quality ("The consumer is our boss, quality is our work and value for money is our goal.")
2. Responsibility ("As individuals, we demand total responsibility from ourselves; as Associates, we support the responsibilities of others.")
3. Mutuality ("A mutual benefit is a shared benefit; a shared benefit will endure.")
4. Efficiency ("We use resources to the full, waste nothing and do only what we can do best.")
5. Freedom ("We need freedom to shape our future; we need profit to remain free.")

Wegmans (a major supermarket chain, one of the largest family businesses in the United States, and a perennial member on the Forbes list of "Best Companies to Work For," referring to "What We Believe"):

At Wegmans, we believe that good people, working toward a common goal, can accomplish anything they set out to do. In this spirit, we set our goal to be the very best at serving the needs of our customers. Every action we take should be made with this in mind. We also believe that we can achieve our goal only if we fulfill the needs of our own people. To the customers and our people we pledge continuous improvement, and we make the commitment: "Every Day You Get Our Best."

S.C. Johnson & Son, Inc. (a family business that started in 1882, now in its fifth generation of family ownership, well known for such products as Windex, Glade Air Freshener, and Pledge, referring to "This we believe"):

Employees: We believe that the fundamental vitality and strength of our worldwide company lies in our people.

Consumer and Users: We believe in earning the enduring goodwill of consumers and users of our products and services.

General Public: We believe in being a responsible leader within the free market economy.

Neighbors and Hosts: We believe in contributing to the well being of the countries and communities where we conduct business.

World Community: We believe in improving international understanding.

Using a Statement of Values

In order to enhance its likelihood of success, a family business should clarify its values and develop an understanding of how those values might be promoted through policy and practice. Consider Nordstrom, Inc., one of this country's great family businesses, and one of the most admired retail businesses in the world. For many years, Nordstrom's employee handbook was a single 5-by-8-inch gray card stating the following:

Welcome to Nordstrom

We're glad to have you with our Company. Our number one goal is to provide outstanding customer service. Set both your personal and professional goals high. We have great confidence in your ability to achieve them.

Nordstrom Rules: Rule #1: Use best judgment in all situations. There will be no additional rules.

Please feel free to ask your department manager, store manager, or division general manager any question at any time.

In their fascinating book, *The Nordstrom Way*, authors Robert Spector and Patrick McCarthy write that this rule sounds simple enough and "probably doesn't differ very much from thousands of other companies: Take care of the customer; do your job; blah, blah, blah. But what sets Nordstrom apart is that it translates these pronouncements into performance; it converts precepts into profits."[16] Nordstrom gives its employees the freedom to make decisions that are consistent with its core value of providing great customer service, even publicizing acts of service that are above and beyond the call of duty as "heroic." Spector and McCarthy describe the following example of a heroic act by a Nordstrom employee:

A [Nordstrom] customer, who was about to catch a flight at Seattle-Tacoma Airport, inadvertently left her airline ticket on a counter in one of Nordstrom's women's apparel departments. Discovering the ticket, her Nordstrom sales associate immediately phoned the airline and asked the service representative if she could track down the customer at the airport and write her another ticket. No, she could not. So the Nordstrom salesperson jumped into a cab, rode out to the airport (at her own expense), located the customer, and delivered the ticket herself. (Nordstrom later reimbursed her for the cab fare.)[17]

One can imagine the customer loyalty the heroic employee created that day.

Empowering employees to make decisions consistent with a company's articulated principles creates an energized and motivated workforce. In an interesting article in *Harvard Business Review* on how organizations can create sustainable performance, Professors Gretchen Spreitzer and Christine Porath write that "[e]mployees at every level are energized by the ability to make decisions that affect their work. Empowering them in this way gives them a greater sense of control, more say in how things get done, and more opportunities for learning."[18]

Developing a Statement of Values

There is no formulaic approach to writing a statement of values. However, done well, any approach used should be fun and motivating. One way to develop a value statement is to use the following seven-step approach:

Step 1. Ask family members (and key stakeholders) to think about what they believe are the values most important to their family business.

Step 2. Have each individual share those values and record them on a flip chart.

Step 3. Ask each individual to consider the list generated by the entire group and identify what they believe are the three most important values.

Step 4. Count the votes each listed value receives and create a short list comprised of the top five vote-getting values.

Step 5. Discuss the short list of values and consider whether any of the family business's core values have been neglected.

Step 6. Finally, after robust discussion on the list generated, ask the group if that list of values captures the business's highest priorities and overall culture. If so, memorialize and publish the statement of values on the company's website, brochures, etc.

Step 7. Agree that, going forward, actions and decisions must be consistent with these agreed-upon values.

Developing a Separate Statement of Family Values (or a Code of Conduct)

Families in business together are best served when they understand and support the needs of both business *and* family. With respect to values, families might consider creating both a statement of values that is focused on business operations as well as a statement of values (sometimes referred to as a Code of Conduct) focused on ensuring that family relationships are respected, keeping the goal of fostering strong relationships a priority.

Articulated, family-based value statements typically endorse values intended to clarify what behaviors are acceptable. Family members in business together should take the time to identify their most important core values and find opportunities to reaffirm them, practicing them consistently and educating new family members as to their significance. Some values that can be particularly important for families to adopt and use include:

1. **Integrity**: a commitment to doing what is right.
2. **Relationships**: a commitment to building and improving relationships through mutual understanding, respect, support, and compassion for each other.
3. **Communication**: a commitment to transparently share information within the family.
4. **Accountability**: a commitment to accepting responsibility for actions without excuses or justifications.
5. **Continuous Improvement**: a commitment to constantly seeking to improve through study and experience.
6. **Happiness**: a commitment to seeking an appropriate balance between work and play, pursuing individual passions, and always appreciating blessings.
7. **Disagreement**: a commitment to trying to resolve interpersonal problems directly with the other person involved before seeking alternative solutions.

A code of conduct should also address the consequences for breaching the code—perhaps, for example, a warning, then a modest consequence, and, ultimately, for a third (or repeated) breach, a severance of the working relationship with the family business.

A Mission Statement

An organizational mission statement is typically intended to answer the following three questions: (1) What does the organization do?, (2) Whom does it do it for?, and (3) Why does it do it? The answers to these questions can both help a business distinguish itself from other businesses and, most importantly, keep it focused on its most important initiatives. Individuals might also benefit from developing a personal mission statement, which can help them stay focused on "what they are called to do."

While there is no single right way to develop a family business mission statement, one approach would be to ask family members and stakeholders to think of words and phrases that answer the following questions:

1. What are our core strengths and competencies?
2. Why do we do what we do?
3. Whom do we do It for? (Who are our customers?)
4. What are we especially good at?
5. What added value do we provide to our customers?

Whether for organizational or personal use, a mission statement can help guide action to accomplish initiatives, plans, and programs as well as guide decisions about what business and personal opportunities to pursue. Good mission statements can help shape strategic direction and align decisions and actions to that end. Efforts consistent with the mission should drive accomplishments that will help bring about a desired future state. In a family business, a mission statement should reflect a clear commitment to a common purpose held by the family and its stakeholders.

Examples of Mission Statements

Good mission statements are often short (two or three sentences) and inspire passion and commitment to the stated core purpose. Consider the following examples from well-known and admired family businesses.

JM Family Enterprises, Inc. (the world's largest independent distributor of Toyotas and Scions, and the world's largest-volume Lexus dealership): "To be the premier provider of quality products and services. To accomplish our goal, we build mutually rewarding relationships with our customers, associates, business partners and the community."

The Walt Disney Company: "The mission of the Walt Disney Company is to be one of the world's leading producers and providers of entertainment and information. Using our portfolio of brands to differentiate our content, services, and consumer products, we seek to develop the most creative, innovative, and profitable entertainment experiences and related products in the world."

A Vision Statement

A vision statement describes a desired future state, sometimes five or ten years away, sometimes even further out. Unlike a dream or wishful thinking, a vision should be based on reality and realistic possibilities that can be achieved by successfully executing a well-developed strategic plan. A good vision statement can help to ensure that all company stakeholders are working toward a common purpose.

Dr. Sanjiv Chopra, comparing "visioning" with "dreaming," writes:

> Great leaders have dreams—and they are decisive. They have a vision for what is possible. Paraphrasing a line from *Back to Methuselah*, by George Bernard Shaw, the U.S. attorney-general and presidential candidate Robert F. Kennedy once said, "There are those that look at things the way they are, and ask why? I dream of things that never were, and ask why not."[19]

When articulating a desired image of the future, family businesses should strive to find a healthy balance between what is exciting and what is realistic, avoiding statements that set the bar unnecessarily low or unrealistically high.

It might prove useful for families to consider the four basic types of vision statements identified by one commentator:

1. **Quantitative Visions**. For example, Wal-Mart's vision in 1990 to become a $125 billion company by the year 2000 or Microsoft's vision in the 1990s to put a "computer on every desk and in every home; all running Microsoft software."

2. **David-versus-Goliath Visions**. For example, Nike's vision in the 1960s to "crush Adidas."

3. **Role-Model Visions**. For example, Stanford's vision in the 1940s to become "the Harvard of the West."

4. **Internal Transformations Visions**. For example, General Electric's vision in the 1980s to "become number one or two in every market we serve and revolutionize this company to have the strengths of a big company combined with the leanness and agility of a small company."[20]

A Note on Vision versus Mission

A vision statement seeks to describe what a company wants to achieve in the future. In contrast, a mission statement seeks to describe how this vision will be realized. In other words, if a family business successfully executes its mission today, it might realistically hope to make its vision a reality tomorrow.

Examples of Vision Statements

Delaware North Companies Vision Statement: "To become the preferred provider of products and services that foresee and satisfy the needs of customers, balancing the highest level of satisfaction consistent with maximizing returns to stakeholders." (Delaware North is one of the most admired family-owned hospitality management and food service companies in the world, and it is approaching its 100th anniversary.)

General Motors Vision Statement: "GM's vision is to be the world leader in transportation products and related services. We will earn our customers' enthusiasm through continuous improvement driven by the integrity, teamwork, and innovation of GM people."

Amazon.com's Vision Statement: "Our vision is to be earth's most customer-centric company; to build a place where people can come to find and discover anything they might want to buy online."

Developing a Vision Statement

The process to develop a vision statement is much like that used to develop a mission statement and statement of values. Those working on developing a vision statement might find it helpful to answer the following questions:

1. How would we like to look five (or ten) years from now?
2. How can we continue to differentiate ourselves from the competition?
3. What kind of company do we want to be?

Additional suggestions to keep in mind when developing a vision statement are:

1. **Make it inspiring**. Because one of the key purposes of a vision statement is to motivate a team, a vision statement should describe an inspiring future.
2. **Make it measurable**. Consider how the vision statement might be drafted so that stakeholders will know whether progress is being made.

3. **Make it clear**. Make the vision statement easily understood to help promote focus.
4. **Make it fit**. Perhaps most importantly, a vision statement must authentically fit with the family business's unique culture.

Updating Your Value, Mission, and Vision Statements

A family business may wish to revisit and revise its value, mission, and vision statements from time to time. Mission statements, reflecting a company's current reality, may need to be revised based on changing times and circumstances. Vision statements, intending to envision an inspiring future often many years away, tend to last longer. Value statements are generally considered so fundamental to an organization that, unlike goals, mission, and vision, they might never change.

Alignment of Values, Mission, and Vision

Family businesses and their advisers can no longer ignore the importance of clarifying and committing to values, a mission, and a vision. These core principles affect people's focus on goals, actions, information, and concerns as well as their attitudes, decisions, choices, and behavior.[21]

Too many families allow their members to work in the family business without imposing any requirements or preconditions. However, having stakeholders whose behavior is inconsistent with the articulated core principles can drain other stakeholders of energy and enthusiasm. Indeed, such a practice can expose the family to great risk. This should be replaced with an approach that considers whether there is a good fit between an individual family member and the business. "Fit" in this instance is not only a function of traditional business factors, but also whether the family member's personally held principles are consistent with other stakeholders' core principles. Assuming a healthy alignment between individual and organizational principles, a family can find ways to overcome many obstacles together. When family members lack alignment between personal and business principles, the family would be wise to consider supporting those members in pursuing their personal mission and vision in some fashion outside of the family business.

One observer, writing about the founder and former CEO of Infosys, N.R. Narayana Murthy, who endeavored to keep rules simple because they are easier to understand, easier to communicate, and simpler to follow, noted:

Even in small matters, Murthy keeps to these principles: Each month he writes a check to cover his personal calls on the office telephone, and he also pays for his personal use of the photocopying machine. Other top executives do the same. "We wanted to found a company that was different from any other we had seen," says Murthy.[22]

Documenting Core Principles in a Family Constitution

The value, mission, and vision statements stand as the core principles of a family business. All other documents a family might agree upon should be philosophically consistent with these core principles. As such, it is important to memorialize these collective, core principles so that they can be referred to and used in making decisions. Central to helping a family move from a P/E Low culture where decisions are ad hoc and inconsistent, these guiding principles function like a constitution and are often collected and organized in what is often called a "family constitution."

The importance of creating a family constitution has already received some recognition in scholarly legal publications. For example, Linda McClain, professor of law at Boston University, discussed the important role family mission statements and family constitutions can play, noting:

> One reported impetus for families drafting family constitutions is a perception that an important relationship between families and other institutions of civil society and government is askew: Because these other institutions are no longer serving as generators or supporters of values—and are even hostile to families—families must define their own ends and values.
>
> Another impetus for family constitution making is the premise that the family, as an organization, should structure itself as do other organizations: By analogy to how other organizations operate, the family must have a constitution or a mission statement. These analogies to the polity and to the corporation raise significant questions about the contemporary functions of families, by comparison with other institutions of civil society and with government, and about the architecture, or infrastructure, of civil society.[23]

Taking the time to develop core principles, memorializing them in a family constitution, and integrating these principles by remaining true to them, can be one of the most important steps a family can take in creating a sustainable family business operating at P/E Max.

The impact of Success Factor 4—P/E Max—is reflected in Figure 11.

Figure 11: The Impact of Success Factor 4—P/E Max

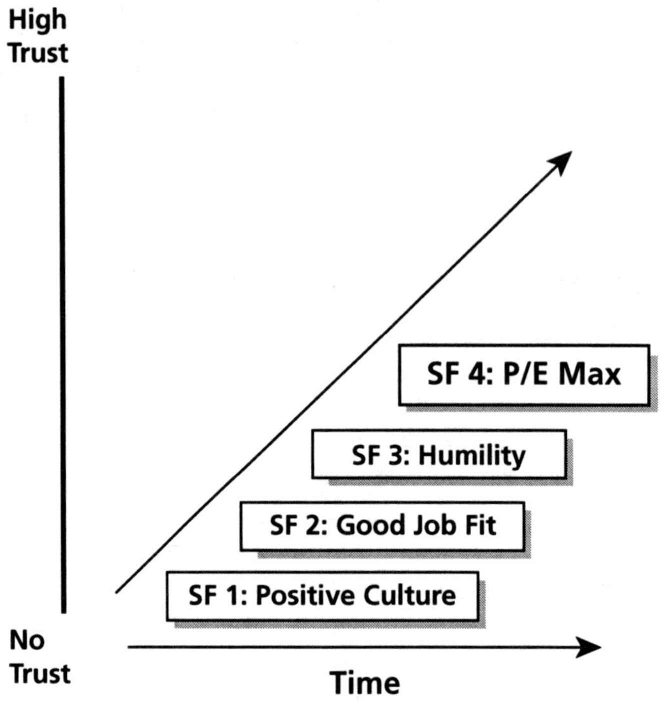

High Trust

SF 4: P/E Max

SF 3: Humility

SF 2: Good Job Fit

SF 1: Positive Culture

No Trust

Time

In addition to articulating their core values, mission, and vision, families are also well served by adopting a variety of policies to enhance a principle-based decision-making culture. Some of these policies, such as a compensation policy, a "perks policy," or a policy that defines eligibility for working in the family business, will be considered in chapter 9.

Quotations

"As you live your values, your sense of identity, integrity, control, and inner-directedness will infuse you with both exhilaration and peace. You will define yourself from within, rather than by people's opinions or by comparisons to others. 'Wrong' and 'right' will have little to do with being found out."

Stephen Covey

"When your values are clear to you, making decisions becomes easier."

Roy Disney

"As long as the world is turning and spinning, we're gonna be dizzy and we're gonna make mistakes."

Mel Brooks

"Leaders with principle are less likely to get bullied and pushed around because they can draw clear lines in the sand. The softest pillow is a clear conscience."

N.R. Narayana Murthy, founder and former CEO,
Infosys Technologies Ltd. (NASDAQ: INFY)

Governance Redux | 7

"The first principle is that you must not fool yourself, and you are the easiest person to fool."

Richard P. Feynman, Nobel Prize–winning physicist

Background: Failure Factor 5 (Insular Perspectives)

While earlier material in this book has highlighted some of the ways in which our brain's judgment can be distorted, including by fight-or-flight tendencies, imperfect memories, and attention deficits, family businesses face still another challenge related to the nature of our brains' functionality: our hereditary tendency to make irrational, biased, and hasty decisions.

These tendencies, the subject of popular books like *Blink* by Malcolm Gladwell, *Freakonomics* by Steven D. Levitt and Stephen J. Dubner, and *Fooled by Randomness* by Nassim Nicholas Taleb, help explain why many of us ignore life-threatening risks like texting while driving, whereas we are more afraid of statistically smaller risks, such as flying on airplanes. *Discover Magazine's* feature on the subject, published in fall 2012, reported:

> We do many amazing things with our brains. Some of those things seem at first to be amazingly dumb. For example, we

believe things to "feel" correct, even when we have plenty of evidence to the contrary. We are terrified of shark attacks, but the risk they pose is actually tiny. Domestic cattle kill dozens more Americans each year. . . .

Equipped with such large, powerful brains, how do we go so wrong? These errors aren't stupid . . . they're systematic—the product of cognitive strategies that help us evade danger, find food, and perform other feats essential for survival.

. . . Sometimes, however, those quick but primitive mental habits get in our way. They supplant more sophisticated reasoning, and the result looks like a dumb mistake. Neuroscientists are beginning to understand why we jump to conclusions, fail to consider evidence, or resort to bias and conjecture instead of sticking to the facts.[1]

Daniel Kahneman, a Nobel Prize–winning professor of psychology at Princeton, describes the hasty risk-based assessments humans are prone to making by observing, "We are often confident even when we are wrong, and an objective observer is more likely to detect our errors than we are."[2]

As the previous chapter highlighted, clarifying and committing to core principles can dramatically help to minimize inconsistent (unprincipled), biased (expedient), and irrational decisions. However, I have found that our tendency toward making biased and irrational decisions is so pervasive that families are sometimes unable to interpret how their own core principles should be applied in practice when faced with challenging issues. This results in an occasional inability to make smart, principled decisions and consequently the failure to mediate interpersonal differences. A family member who makes irrational or biased decisions may lose the trust of other family members and stakeholders.

To prevent these irrational decisions, insight from outside the family is sometimes required. Moreover, the knowledge, experience, judgment, and relationships that is required to successfully navigate competitive waters is vast and often beyond what a family can access from only family members.

Failure Factor 5 is intended to describe both the problematic decisions resulting from our unchecked tendency to make predictably irrational decisions as well as the tendency to make bad business decisions because of a lack of education, experience, and insight. Family businesses are well served by implementing Success Factor 5: creating an effective board of directors, which can be of great help by offering knowledgeable, wise, and unbiased advice.

Robust and constructive communication within a family business is a critical success factor, particularly as the size of a family expands. However, since it can become unmanageable to provide all family stakeholders with a seat on the company's board of directors, another mechanism must be established to ensure that all family members have an opportunity for input. This objective can be met by establishing what is often referred to as a "family council," complementing business governance by serving as the forum for family governance. Accordingly, complementing a board of directors with a family council is a second aspect of Success Factor 5. This chapter considers both the benefits and mechanics of establishing a board of directors for governance of the business, a family council for governance of the family, and how the two governance vehicles can cooperatively work hand in hand.

> Traditionally, a board of directors is a creature of corporate law. Limited liability companies (LLCs), which contemplate the possibility of a board of managers that might function analogously to a board of directors, have become an increasingly popular form for doing business in recent years. To avoid potential confusion, all references to "boards of directors" in this book should be construed as including "boards of managers" as well.

Benefits of an Effective Board

By lending experience, expertise, and perspective, a board of directors constituted of capable members can provide many benefits to any organization. Having a "professional board"—one that includes some independent (i.e., nonfamily) members—can help a family in business together vet decisions through unbiased filters. This results not only in more thoughtful decisions, but creates yet another mechanism that structurally reinforces feelings of trust and confidence among family members and company employees. Some of the most important benefits particularly relevant to family businesses include (1) expertise, (2) objectivity, (3) accountability, (4) perspective, (5) relationships, (6) credibility, (7) succession, and (8) dispute resolution. Each will be discussed in turn below.

Expertise

Nonfamily directors can bring additional expertise to a family business. This expertise can provide a useful sounding board for a company's leaders on both family and business matters. For example, outside board members can be helpful in offering honest feedback on operational decisions and in helping develop and oversee long-term strategic plans. Bringing different perspectives to a discussion, outside board members can often suggest creative and thoughtful approaches to how best to solve problems and pursue opportunities. Consider Wal-Mart, founded by Sam Walton, controlled by members of his family, and one of the largest family-owned businesses in the United States. While members of the Walton family serve on the company's board of directors, the company benefits from having multiple, highly regarded nonfamily board members.[3]

Capable nonfamily board members can also offer insight and expertise on "family matters." For example, board members can help a family work through a variety of key planning initiatives, such as succession planning or helping resolve an intra-family disagreement. Nonfamily advisers can also help monitor application of a family's core principles and assist in mediating any differences in perspectives if questions arise as to how those core principles should be applied and honored in practice. Nonfamily board members also serve a valuable role as mentors to those tasked with leading the family business into its next generation.

> One study on the influence of family and nonfamily stakeholders on the success of family businesses notes the following:
>
> > Outsider expertise improves the quality of discussions about strategy, improves decision-making, and increases the chances of business survival. . . . [O]utsiders serve as critical "trust catalysts," building bridges between siblings and other subordinates.[4]

Objectivity

Family executives can't always count on getting honest and unbiased advice from family members and employees. Employees may be reluctant to disagree with their employer. Family members might also be uncomfortable disagreeing as a matter of family dynamics. Alternatively, if a family member supports a family executive's decision, it might be difficult for that executive to assess whether that supporting perspective is sound and appropriate or whether it is motivated by an agenda to curry personal favor. Inexperienced professional advisers, including lawyers, accountants, and consultants, may be reluctant to offer objective advice for fear of upsetting a client and sabotaging an important business relationship. Less encumbered, nonfamily board members are particularly well suited to offer not only their expertise and experience, but unbiased and independent advice on critical matters.

> British psychologist Peter Watson conducted a series of experiments in the 1960s concluding that we prefer evidence that confirms and supports our existing beliefs, while ignoring information that could challenge or refute them. This "confirmation bias" can present itself in family businesses in a variety of ways. For example, a family member irresponsible as an adolescent may have matured over the years. Other family members, holding onto a prior perspective, may continue to consider that individual irresponsible, notwithstanding new evidence to the contrary.

Accountability

Professional board members can help family business leaders succeed by asking challenging questions and holding management's feet to the fire. Independent board members are well suited for pointing out behaviors and challenging plans that threaten the business's core principles and operations while providing guidance on how to manage challenging issues in a constructive manner.

As an example, I recently worked with one family business that had a "well-credentialed," nonfamily member serving in a senior executive position. The family was uncertain whether the individual was actually doing a good job or not. I helped the family create a board of directors that included three experienced business professionals who helped establish key performance indicators that were used to confirm that the executive's contribution was weak and didn't justify his continued employment.

Perspective

Company executives often benefit from the additional perspective nonfamily board members might offer on a variety of matters, such as how to best pursue a new opportunity (or whether to pursue it) and how to manage difficult problems. Several years ago, I helped form such a board for one successful family-owned business. Forming this board was precipitated by the founder's interest in getting outside advisers to help him identify and then mentor his successor. We helped the owner establish appropriate criteria for evaluating potential successors based on a variety of metrics, including education, experience, and interpersonal skills. These metrics were used to identify a candidate who seems to be a great fit for this business.

John A. Davis, a senior lecturer in the Entrepreneurial Management program at Harvard Business School and leading authority on family businesses, suggests that helping make "big picture decisions" is the most important board duty. He writes:

> Boards should advise and help senior management think about "big picture" topics important to the company, such as its vision, strategy, growth plans, ability to compete, development of human, financial, and physical resources, strategic relationships, and succession. I like to say that boards should fly at 30,000 feet, meaning that they should think broadly about the company's goals and challenges, concentrate on the big issues facing the company and avoid getting involved in day-to-day management or operations issues.[5]

In the 1970s, Yale University psychology professor Irving Janis studied the propensity of groups, under certain conditions, to make decisions by consensus in order to reduce potential conflict—even at the cost of ignoring

(continued)

realistic and better alternatives. Janis, describing this phenomenon as "groupthink," wrote that the "more amiability and esprit de corps there is among the members of a policy-making ingroup, the greater the danger that independent critical thinking will be replaced by groupthink, which is likely to result in irrational and dehumanizing actions directed against outgroups."[6] In another interesting study, researchers at Duke University calculated that more than 40 percent of our behavior is guided by unconscious habits, not actual decisions. Researchers have learned much about the structure of habits, including how they are based on cues, routines, and rewards. We are often unaware that many of our decisions are "habitual" instead of "thoughtful."[7]

Relationships

Outside board members can also benefit a family business by expanding the network of potential suppliers, customers, sources of capital, professionals, and others who might help the business. For example, a business might benefit from establishing any number of key strategic partnerships, some of which can lead to introductions to a potential acquirer. Nonfamily members often have contacts that are different than those the family has access to, helping identify additional opportunities for the family.

Credibility

Because family members and other stakeholders are not always in a position to evaluate the substantive merits of a CEO's decisions, the importance of how those decisions are perceived is impossible to overestimate. It is not unusual for a CEO to make the very best decision for the company, though it might not be perceived as such by the company's employees or family shareholders as a result of fear-driven bias or misunderstanding. On the other hand, the same decision supported and endorsed by a strong and respected board of directors can provide stakeholders with confidence that the decision is smart and principled. That, in turn, can bolster morale and confidence. Accordingly, one of the most important benefits that a professional board with nonfamily members brings to a family business is credibility.

I once worked with a family business inherited by three brothers. One brother graduated from an Ivy League college and then earned his MBA at one of the top business schools in the country. The other two brothers never graduated from college and didn't work in the family business but collected substantial dividends. Unable to evaluate the merits of their brother's decisions as CEO, and concerned that their dividends were at risk, they used their majority voting control to block many of his initiatives. I sought to organize a board of respected business professionals in order to give the brothers confidence that decisions and actions were smart, fair, and appropriate. Unfortunately, it is not unusual for family business owners to resist such advice because they fear losing control. In this case, I was unable to convince my client that adding nonfamily members to the board would be helpful. In the end, the family continued to quarrel.

Succession

Independent board members might help a family business with respect to succession planning, a subject considered in more detail in chapter 9. For example, an effective board might help identify appropriate criteria for a successor, including minimum educational requirements, experience, and personality profile. The board might also help the family identify whether one or more family members can fill those criteria well or whether the business would be better served by looking to a nonfamily executive. Also, it is not unusual for a family business leader to die or become disabled before a succession has been completed. In those instances, a capable board of directors might help provide interim leadership and guidance while a search for a permanent successor is completed or a decision to sell the business is made.

Dispute Resolution

Effective nonfamily board members can also serve an important role in mediating continuing disagreements and disputes between family members. This role is considered in more detail in chapter 8.

Board of Directors versus Board of Advisers

An issue facing family businesses is whether to form a "board of directors" or a "board of advisers." A board of directors is organized and functions according to laws of the jurisdiction in which the business is organized. An advisory board is neither required nor governed by law, so it can be operated in any manner that the family might want, perhaps voting on some (but not all) particularly key issues or offering "advice" but not actually voting on a decision. Some factors to consider in deciding whether a board of directors or board of advisers makes sense for a particular family business include authority, formality, quality of focus, liability, costs, and fiduciary duties.

Authority

State laws provide shareholders with the authority to appoint individuals to be on their company's board of directors. Directors, in turn, are responsible for overseeing the activities of the corporation on behalf of the shareholders. By contrast, state law does not require advisory boards that are established at the discretion of a company's leaders. Because its authority is discretionary, a CEO has the power not only to choose the members of the advisory board but to replace them or terminate the board without shareholder or member approval.

Formality

Boards of directors are legally required to function in accordance with formal bylaws, which detail such matters as the scope of the board's responsibilities, how often the board meets, and how directors are elected and removed. By contrast, advisory boards are typically far less formal and generally meet whenever requested to do so by the CEO.

Quality of Focus

As a practical matter, a board of directors may be more motivated to help a company succeed because it has legally dischargeable duties to shareholders and the members are generally compensated for their service. Also, since directors typically receive much more information from the company than advisory board members, they are generally able to make better decisions. Since being held liable for the advice they provide is unlikely, advisory board members may give less attention to the information they receive than a board of directors would. Also, advisers serving without compensation may lack the same focus that compensated board members bring to the family.

Liability

Members of a board of directors have legal duties and responsibilities to the company and owners they serve. If they ignore those duties, they may have liability exposure to shareholders, employees, and third parties. Accordingly, it is not unusual for companies to provide board members with directors and officers insurance, protecting them from personal liability. By contrast, advisory board members generally do not face personal liability for mistakes made while advising the company. As a result, potential advisers might be more inclined to serve on an advisory board than on a board of directors. If the cost of insurance is too expensive for a company, creating a board of advisers, thereby eliminating the need for insurance, may be a sensible option.

Cost

Boards of directors are typically more expensive than advisory boards due to the higher compensation paid to members in consideration for the legal responsibility associated with the role. Because meetings can be infrequent and comparatively short, it is not unusual for advisory board members to serve without any compensation. In some instances, trusted members of either a board of directors or advisers might receive a small equity stake in the company.

Fiduciary Duties

Board members owe fiduciary duties to the company and its shareholders. While this helps ensure a high level of focus and attention, board members may occasionally find themselves feeling conflicted by simultaneously serving as advisers to a company CEO who wants to pursue a particular matter that board members disagree with. By contrast, a board of advisers has no such technical fiduciary duties and can more comfortably focus on serving the CEO. As a result, a member of a board of directors might have a responsibility to proactively intervene in a situation he or she believes is being mismanaged, while a member of a board of advisers might think twice about intervening if the subject is a delicate one and there is no legal responsibility to speak up.

These are important differences and care should be given to whether a family business would be best served by forming a board of directors or a board of advisers. A board of advisers may be somewhat easier to create than a board of directors because members can be recruited to serve only as long as needed and they don't need to be reassured about how they will be safeguarded from potential claims brought by dissatisfied shareholders. On the other hand, a formal board of directors can often add greater value to the family for the reasons noted above.

In his best-selling book, *Predictably Irrational*, Dan Ariely, a professor at Duke University, writes:

> Our minds and bodies are capable of amazing acts . . . We can master chess. We can recognize thousands of faces without confusing them. We can produce music, literature, technology, and art—and the list goes on. . . .
>
> Although a feeling of awe at the capability of humans is clearly justified, there is a large difference between a deep sense of admiration and the assumption that our reasoning abilities are perfect. In fact, this book is about human irrationality—about our distance from perfection. I believe that recognizing where we depart from the ideal is an important part of the quest to truly understand ourselves, and one that promises many practical benefits. Understanding irrationality is important in everyday actions and decisions, and for understanding how we design our environment and the choices it presents to us.[8]

Common Reasons Family Businesses Avoid Forming Professional Boards

Notwithstanding the great benefit nonfamily members bring to a board of directors, most family businesses are quintessentially private organizations and tend to avoid including nonfamily members. As a result, many family businesses create a board of directors comprised solely of family members that serves no practical purpose beyond satisfying technical legal requirements. These boards usually meet infrequently, if at all, sometimes approving all matters only by written resolutions. Without the mandated reporting requirements associated with their public company counterparts, directors of family businesses are more likely to maintain a shroud of secrecy on issues that they wish to keep private not only from the public but from owners as well. This culture of privacy and confidentiality, however, creates a culture of resistance to the practice of creating and relying on a board of directors (or a board of advisers) that includes nonfamily members who can offer not only relevant expertise but objective and nonbiased perspectives as well.

Lacking independent outside board members, business leaders of family enterprises often make decisions that are arbitrary, biased, or unwise.

Many family businesses resist advice to form a professional board of directors because they fear that nonfamily board members would be expensive, that it would be embarrassing to expose family secrets to nonfamily members, or that an important measure of control would be lost to outsiders. However, in practice, I have never seen a quality board member who didn't create more value than the board fees charged or wasn't sensitive to family issues and respecting family control. Reflecting the value added by a professional board, I don't know a single family business with nonfamily board members that would now consider operating in any other way.

Structuring the Board

There is no single best way to form a board, and each family business should determine for itself what makes the most sense for its particular circumstances. A family should keep in mind that its needs and interests might change over time and it will always be free to change the board as its needs dictate. Subject to such qualifications, families might be guided by the considerations that follow.

Number of Board Members

Some families prefer starting with one nonfamily member to become comfortable having someone in this role. I have found that having up to three nonfamily members can be a good number—not too large so as to create stress or unnecessary formality, but enough voices to add enhanced expertise, perspective, and credibility to important decisions. Smaller boards not dominated by family members tend to work better. For example, if a family business is considering expanding into international markets and investing a substantial amount of money to make that happen, it might be reassuring to get several well-respected businessmen supporting the initiative. Regardless of how many board members are asked to serve, they should all be capable and independent, and not inclined to rubber-stamp a CEO's decisions out of friendship.

Decision Making

A board of directors should enjoy working together to promote the interests of the company and its owners. Ideally, discussions will lead to consensus on how to act. However, consensus is not always achievable, so rules on how decisions should be made are helpful and, if it is a board of directors, such rules are even required by state law. Typically, a quorum of the board of directors is required before proceeding. Establishing that at least half of the board members are present to satisfy quorum requirements is common. It is also common practice to provide that board decisions are to be decided by a simple majority vote. It is good practice to require a board member to recuse him or herself from a vote on a matter on which he or she is particularly interested.

> One of the big challenges for boards of directors in family businesses is how to strike a smart balance between the interests of the company and those of its owners. While one might think that those interests should overlap, that isn't always the case in the real world, particularly, for example, when owners would prefer larger dividends or distributions for their lifestyle but the company could use those funds for operating capital. The family and board can benefit from clarifying their shared principles around uses of capital and then entrust business leadership to use good judgment to support actions and decisions that strengthen the company and enhance shareholder value in a manner consistent with those principles.

Terms

Family businesses are free to function and operate as they see fit. If they are blessed with great board members, there is no reason to require them to limit their contribution to a particular term in office. Indeed, long-tenured and loyal board members can create enormous value because of their familiarity with the business and the family. However, for family businesses that are just getting started with a board, establishing term limits on board service can provide a graceful mechanism to address non-productive board members. Having term limits can also provide a similarly graceful mechanism to recruit new board members who might bring additional value to the business, based on the family's changing circumstances. The injection of new energy and ideas can help create new opportunities for family businesses.

Number of Meetings

The frequency and formality of meetings is, again, a function of a number of factors, including board size, board responsibilities, culture, and need. Having a sufficient number of meetings so the board members get comfortable working with each other is important. That typically requires full board meetings on at least a quarterly basis—a frequency that will also give board members the ability to stay updated on material developments within the business.

Compensating Board Members

Board members should be compensated for their board service, including attending board and committee meetings. Out-of-pocket expenses associated with attending board meetings should also be reimbursed. While it is customary for publicly traded companies to compensate board members with stock or cash, family businesses generally compensate their board members with cash only so as not to dilute family ownership. Occasionally a form of "phantom equity" is used to give directors a practical way to participate in equity like returns for their contributions. The amount of compensation will typically vary, depending on the size and financial resources of the business.

Committees

In larger and more complex family businesses, it might be helpful to establish board committees to bring focus to particular issues. Typically, committees meet to consider and then recommend policies or action for approval by the entire board. While a family business can create committees for any purpose, some of the more traditional committees include the following:

Finance—to oversee the development of the budget and ensure the implementation and oversight of adequate financial controls;

Human Resources—to oversee the development and implementation of personnel policies and procedures;

Audit—to provide oversight of the quality and integrity of the accounting, auditing, and financial reporting practices of the company;

Compensation—to design the company's compensation and benefits systems, including with respect to incentive compensation for the company's senior executive officers and family members; and

Governance—to provide oversight and direction regarding the functioning and operation of the board, including evaluating the chief executive
officer and overseeing succession planning.

Family Governance

Up to this point, we have focused on how "professionalizing" a family business's
board of directors by adding capable and independent nonfamily members can
provide important benefits. Because family businesses often have more family
members than can be included on an efficient board of directors, particularly
as the size of the family expands, it becomes impractical to provide every family
member with a seat at the table. Moreover, because family members may lack
relevant experience to contribute to the professional functioning of the board of
directors, it may also be unwise.

Without a voice that can be heard, however, excluded family members may
feel increasingly disenfranchised and frustrated. Over time, such feelings can
contribute to diminishing trust in how the business is being run, fueling the likelihood of family conflict. Accordingly, it is important that careful consideration
be given not only to governance of the business but to governance of the family
as well. To that end, families in business together are generally best served by
providing a forum to ensure that family members can learn how their business is
performing, ask questions, make suggestions, and contribute to their business's
success in constructive ways. A family council can help accomplish that objective and establish a family governance system that works hand in hand with the
company's business leaders.

Organizing the Family's Governance

Recognizing the importance of robust communication, many family business
consultants help their clients establish a formal governance structure commonly
known as a "family council." The family council can be used as a forum to ensure
that important information is shared, questions are answered, and minor disputes are resolved before they become major disputes.

Unlike a board of directors, a family council is a creature of family agreement and can be structured and operated in any fashion a family finds useful.
Typically, membership in the council is open to all adult members of the family,
including those who are employed by the business and those who are not. Under
most circumstances, it is a good idea to invite spouses of adult members to join
the family council as well. Members should be encouraged not only to attend
meetings, but also to participate in discussions and speak their minds without

fear of embarrassment or repercussions. Because of the nature of the discussion that takes place, minor children are generally not invited to participate on a regular basis.

Among other matters, I have found family council meetings great forums to:

1. discuss challenges and opportunities to balance work and family;
2. develop uniform guidelines for the employment of family members;
3. discuss the pros and cons of employing spouses in the business;
4. discuss family compensation policies;
5. discuss and understand policies, issues, or decisions that will affect the family;
6. discuss the merits of requiring family members to enter into prenuptial agreements; and
7. discuss succession planning, retirement planning, financial planning, and estate planning.

In short, family councils can promote open communication and education that can help reinforce intra-family trust by nurturing relationships.[9]

To help provide an appropriate level of respect for the institution and to ensure its business is addressed in an organized and disciplined fashion, family councils typically schedule regular meetings with set agendas, rules, and procedures. Family councils may find it helpful to establish formalities similar to those of a board of directors, including designating a chair to organize agendas and facilitate meetings. The chair often serves as the main contact person for family members in between council meetings. Some family councils, particularly as they increase in size with the growth of the family, find it helpful to appoint a secretary of the council to record minutes of meetings.

While every family will need to find the right rhythm for scheduling meetings, it is important that the family meet often enough to gain—and retain—traction as a group. Depending on their needs, families should expect to meet as a council on a regularly scheduled basis, perhaps semiannually, quarterly, or, in some cases, even monthly.

Consistent with the insights from positive psychology considered earlier, thought should be given to how to help ensure that family council meetings are constructive and productive. For example, establishing a code of conduct to help ensure that family concerns are dealt with promptly, empathetically, and collegially can be a good idea. Ideally, at the end of council meetings, family members should feel informed and comfortable on a wide range of family and business issues. Unanimous agreement may not always be possible to achieve, but there should be a consensus on these issues and, at a minimum, a sense that the issues were decided in a principled manner consistent with the family's values, mission, and vision. While the council is a forum to discuss grievances and concerns, the family should strive to ensure that discussions on such subjects do not turn into counterproductive finger pointing and blaming. Perhaps more importantly, families should consider how to allocate more of their time to "possibility seeking" (which can enhance creative thought, energy, camaraderie, and other positive emotions) rather than "problem solving" (which can create fight-or-flight responses that, as previously discussed, can be draining and counterproductive).

Getting Started with a Kick-Off Retreat

Families that are establishing a family council for the first time might consider organizing a kick-off retreat at an off-site meeting facility or as part of a family vacation, creating an aspect of fun along with discussions about business.

Families might realize a variety of benefits from using a facilitator at family council meetings, particularly as the family is establishing its council, including:

1. **Focus**. Having a facilitator allows all family members to listen carefully and become better participants.
2. **Participation**. A facilitator can help ensure that everyone participates and rules of order are respected.
3. **Tone**. Facilitators can help guide discussions in a constructive fashion without having a role in deciding substantive issues.
4. **Education**. Having a professional facilitator as the council is being established can educate a family on how to run effective meetings on their own in the future.
5. **Timeliness**. Facilitated meetings are more likely to stay on schedule and limit time spent on subjects that are not on the agenda.

While it is always important to thoughtfully consider the agenda for a kick-off retreat, common topics include:

1. a discussion of the retreat's purpose and any appropriate ground rules (e.g., no cell phones and no interrupting someone who is speaking);

2. an overview of the business's history that might include a description of major milestones met, challenges faced, and opportunities realized;

3. an overview of the business's operations, including strategy, competition, opportunities, and finances;

4. a discussion of the commitments required to retain and grow a family business, including a related "appreciative discussion" about the opportunities presented as a result of having been born into (or having married into) a family business;

5. working on defining the family's core principles, including a vision statement, mission statement, and statement of values;

6. starting to work on appropriate agreements, policies, and structures, including, for example, what responsibilities the council will have, what responsibilities the board will have, and how the council can most effectively work with the board; and

7. beginning to address the future of the business, including requirements for working in the business, expectations regarding performance, compensation, and promotion.

Ongoing Subjects for the Family Council

After the family council has established its ground rules for working together, its members should meet on a regularly scheduled basis. The purposes of these ongoing meetings might include promoting core principles; developing and amending policies; establishing a code of conduct; serving as a link to the board of directors; and seeking to enhance stakeholders' happiness.

Promoting Core Principles

Family council meetings are good forums for finding ways to continually reiterate the importance of the family's core values, mission, and vision through discussions that include examples of how they have been used as well as questions about how they might be applied in particular circumstances. Also, the family might, on occasion, find it helpful to update core principles as a result of changing family or business dynamics.

Developing and Amending Policies

Families might usefully determine specific policies that, consistent with their core principles, can help bring sharp clarity to particular aspects of how a family wants to run its business. For example, I have found it helpful for families to develop policies that:

1. establish standards for minimum education and experience necessary before a family member is eligible to work in the business;
2. establish policies that seek to balance running a business professionally, while providing opportunities to family members to work in the business;
3. establish a policy for continuing education for those family members who choose to work in the family business;
4. establish a policy to determine when dividends or distributions are made;
5. establish a succession policy that includes criteria to be used for selecting a successor, as well as when succession will take place;
6. establish a dispute resolution policy;
7. establish a policy on family philanthropy;
8. establish a policy on stock ownership issues; and
9. establish a policy dealing with conflicts of interest.

Establishing a Code of Conduct

A code of conduct is a written document that is designed to provide guidelines for behaviors to promote collegiality between family members and other stakeholders, and to help ensure that differences in perspectives can be constructively reconciled. Codes are generally intended to establish expectations regarding how family members will behave both inside and outside of the business. Beyond helping to guide behavior, having an agreed-upon written code of conduct helps hold family members accountable for their behaviors.

Some families simply opt for the "golden rule" when agreeing to a code of conduct: "Do unto others what you would like others to do unto you." Other families find it helpful to have a more detailed list of "dos and don'ts" that are tailored to fit the particular values and needs of the organization.

The following is an example of a code of conduct:

Sample Family Code of Conduct

All family members agree to:

1. Deal with family members with honesty, candor, respect, and love.
2. Allow others to express their points of view without interruption.

(continued)

3. If necessary, disagree without being disagreeable.
4. Be open to constructive feedback.
5. Address any problem directly with the person creating the problem before asking a third person to intervene.
6. Make decisions consistently with the family's values, mission, vision, and stated policies.
7. Act in accordance with the decisions that are made by the board of directors and family council.
8. Respect decisions made by other family members that are consistent with their duties and authorities.
9. Refrain from criticizing another family member in public.

An excellent long-form example of a code of conduct can be found on the Carlson Company's website at http://www.carlson.com/cdc-cms/pdf/ Carlson%20Code%20of%20Business%20Conduct%20and%20Ethics.pdf.
    Carlson is one of the largest family businesses in the world, with over $38 billion in annual sales and operations in more than 150 countries and territories.

Serving as a Link to the Board of Directors

The family council ordinarily serves as the primary link between the family and the company's board of directors and senior executive, ensuring that family members are regularly updated about the plans and performance of the business. In fulfilling this function, the council often designates one or two members to serve as its representatives on the board of directors. The council also typically considers and suggests possible candidates for board membership.

Pursuing Happiness

Consistent with the insights considered in chapter 4 on the importance of finding strong fits between family members and any role they might play in a family business, the family council can provide a forum for ongoing education and discussions designed to help each family member better understand their unique interests, passions, and circumstances so that their individual dreams and ambitions can be pursued to the fullest extent possible.

The Family Constitution

If the family council focuses on only a fraction of the planning opportunities suggested above, it will have created a variety of important documents, such as a statement of values, mission and vision statements, core policies, and a code of conduct. In order to both keep track of these documents and ensure that they are treated with respect, it has become common practice to formally organize these documents into what is often referred to as a "family constitution."

Having a family constitution that memorializes various roles and rules can help ensure that family members are all on the same page. This, in turn, can help prevent misunderstandings and conflict.

If thoughtfully conceived, the process of preparing a family constitution can be fun and, at the same time, can help to involve family members in the family business and enhance unity. To that end, the process of working together to create a family constitution can be as important as the actual document produced. Learning to work together and create agreed-upon norms of family behavior, while having the opportunity to plan for the future, can be invaluable.

In general, unlike shareholder agreements, family constitutions are not contractually enforceable documents. A breach of a rule or policy does not create an actionable offense. Nevertheless, it is expected that family members who participate in the family council will honor its decisions and respect the agreements set forth in the family constitution. Accordingly, the family should give some thought to the consequences for disregarding the constitutional provisions, which might progressively range from warnings to removal from the family council to, potentially, removal from the family business as well.

There are no requirements for what might be included within a family constitution, nor is there any single right way to prepare such a document. Because of its importance for both current and future generations, families often find that its contents are best developed over a period of time and over the course of several meetings. Once drafted, families should consider reviewing it on a regular basis and updating it as appropriate.

The impact on intra-family trust resulting from Success Factor 5, constituting effective governance structures within a family business, is highlighted in Figure 12.

Figure 12: The Impact of Success Factor 5—Functional Governance

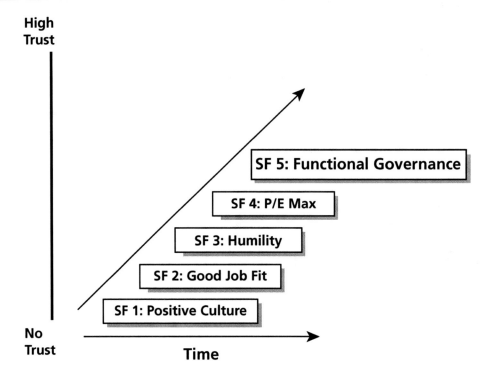

Quotations

"To know that we know what we know, and that we do not know what we do not know, that is true knowledge."

Confucius

"The only real security that a man can have in this world is a reserve of knowledge, experience and ability."

Henry Ford

"The smart ones ask when they don't know. And, sometimes, when they do."

Malcolm Forbes

"Do not be inaccessible. None is so perfect that he does not need at times the advice of others."

Baltasar Gracián

"He that won't be counseled can't be helped."

Benjamin Franklin

"It is the dull man who is always sure, and the sure man who is always dull."

H.L. Mencken

"Friendly counsel cuts off many foes."

William Shakespeare

Conflict Preemption 8

"No matter how thin you slice it, there will always be two sides."

Baruch Spinoza

Background: Failure Factor 6 (Limited Repertoire of Techniques to Prevent and Manage Conflict)

The suggestions contained in the preceding chapters are designed to promote constructive disagreements. However, they are neither designed nor intended to harmonize individual family members' perspectives to ensure that there is always unanimous agreement on matters. As a practical matter, family members will always continue to have different views.

Differences in opinions can actually be a sign of a strong family business, where individuals are encouraged to think openly and creatively. Inevitable differences are a healthy and natural consequence of high-functioning teams that are sharing opinions to benefit the organization. Many times, resolving such differences results in a better decision or work product than would have been made had there not been a robust discussion. As Walter Lippmann once observed, "where all think alike, no one thinks very much."

I firmly believe that "two heads are better than one," and that inevitable differences in opinions can lead, through constructive conversations, to enhanced quality decisions. Sometimes, differences among family members are not so easily reconciled. Nevertheless, they can be handled in a variety of constructive ways, including through direct conversations, third-party mediation, or voluntary separation of one or more family members from the business.

Unfortunately, without proper training and education, differences of opinion within a family business are often mishandled, creating problems that threaten the business's long-term sustainability.

I have found it helpful to distinguish between "disagreements," often simply a signal of healthy communication among family business stakeholders, and "conflict," a state in which such differences are no longer being constructively resolved and family dynamics are unhealthy. By the time a family is trying to resolve conflict, interventions are often challenging and problematic because the situation has already been mishandled, making subsequent disagreements increasingly harder to resolve constructively. Where trust, cohesion, and family dynamics have already deteriorated, family members may find it impossible to reconcile their differences.

Failure Factor 6 describes the existing planning paradigm in which families in business together spend an inordinate amount of time and money with their professional advisers defining and documenting their dispute resolution mechanism of choice. While such planning no doubt serves important purposes, families in business together would be better served by bringing into sharper focus methods of how to disagree constructively and preempt conflict. Accordingly, this chapter considers a variety of mechanisms that acknowledge the inevitability of intra-family disagreement so that, when it does occur, families have a plan to address it constructively, promptly, and successfully.

The Benefits of Constructive Disagreement

"Majority decisions tend to be made without engaging the systematic thought and critical thinking skills of the individuals in the group.... Research shows that the decisions of a group as a whole are more thoughtful and creative when there is minority dissent than when it is absent." Philip G. Zimbardo, *The Lucifer Effect: Understanding How Good People Turn Evil*[1]

Irving Janis famously coined the term "groupthink" to describe the phenomenon of a group coming to a unanimous decision despite the existence of facts suggesting that another decision would be better. Janis, a professor of psychology at Yale in the early 1970s, researched the chain of events that led up to

U.S.-trained soldiers' attempt to overthrow Fidel Castro's Cuban government in the failed Bay of Pigs invasion in 1961. According to Janis' theory, President Kennedy wanted to overthrow Castro and his advisers knew it. As a result, instead of openly and authentically considering and discussing available information that might have suggested another course of action, the group jumped to conclusions that supported Kennedy's decision to invade Cuba rather than challenging him and, potentially, making a more strategically sound decision. The group's unreflective decision put the United States on the brink of war with Russia.

Another famous example of groupthink involved the Challenger space shuttle disaster. It was reported that an engineer knew before takeoff about a faulty part of the shuttle, an O-ring, but in order to avoid negative publicity, other engineers, who shared the concern, convinced themselves that the issue was manageable and decided to proceed with the launch anyway. That decision resulted in the tragic explosion of the shuttle only 73 seconds after launch, killing all seven members of the shuttle crew. A presidential commission appointed to investigate the explosion determined that NASA's decision-making process was a key factor in the accident.[2]

Janis identified a number of problems with decisions reached as a result of groupthink, including incomplete consideration of options, failure to examine risk, bias in processing available information, and failure to consider contingency plans. These problems can prove lethal to any business. Ira Bryck, director of the University of Massachusetts at Amherst Family Business Center, considered this subject and, after noting the miserable failure rate of family businesses, described how groupthink can put a family business at risk:

> [T]here is a tendency [among family businesses] to become frozen by (1) imagining [they are] invulnerable, ignoring danger and risk (2) collectively rationalizing [their] decisions, discrediting minority thinking (3) assuming [they] are morally correct, ignoring ethical consequences (4) stereotyping [their] rivals, ignoring their wisdom (5) viewing opposition as disloyalty (6) withholding . . . dissenting views (7) then perceiving falsely that everyone agrees (8) and protecting the group from adverse information that might threaten [its] complacency.[3]

Seeking to promote "group wisdom" rather than "groupthink," Bryck warns that consistently being on the same page can be a major warning sign. Groupthink may easily arise within a family business since many are started as entrepreneurial ventures with the founder calling all the shots. Founders tend to be very hands-on, uncertain about whom to trust, and very involved in controlling all aspects of their company's operations. Such a "command and control" leadership style can easily breed groupthink, as employees may be reluctant to speak candidly for fear of losing their jobs. The consequences of groupthink in such circumstances are also considered in chapter 7, which notes the importance of constituting a board of directors or advisers that includes nonfamily members, who are more likely to disagree with a founder because they have less to lose.

Janis and others who have studied groupthink offer a variety of suggestions that can be tailored for use by family businesses faced with important decisions, including:

1. Family leaders should avoid stating their preference at the outset of a discussion.
2. As many ideas as possible should be encouraged by allotting time to brainstorm. For particularly sensitive subjects, consideration should be given to gathering feedback anonymously.
3. Identifying and evaluating the pros and cons of all options should be encouraged. Consider asking a family member to serve as "devil's advocate" and challenge the proposed option or ideas of the group.
4. Arrive at a solution only after appropriately considering all options—at which point all family members should, ideally, indicate their support for the decision and commit to following through as required.

While family businesses can find quality brainstorming to be enormously helpful because group wisdom is more likely to result in a better decision than groupthink, not all family business discussions are neatly resolved by unanimous agreement. There will be times, of course, when family members continue to disagree on what is the best path forward. In order to help keep those instances from getting out of hand, families would benefit by applying scientifically derived insights on how differences can be constructively resolved.

Constructive Disagreement

For reasons discussed earlier, humans seem hardwired for disagreement. If not handled sensitively, disagreements can quickly spiral into destructive conflicts. In many respects, what makes the difference is often not the particular issue being resolved but how the decision-making process is handled. Dr. Anil Menon, an expert on marketing and a former faculty member at Emory University's Roberto C. Goizueta Business School, surveyed 236 marketing executives concerning conflict that accompanied new product introduction in their companies. In studying the circumstances that promoted both constructive and destructive discussions, consistent with the lessons of groupthink and group wisdom, Menon found that:

> Conflict was constructive when managers guided discussions that included vigorous challenging of ideas, beliefs, and assumptions; when they encouraged people to consider new ideas from other departments; when they encouraged their own people to offer ideas to others; and when they encouraged the free expression of opinions and feelings.

Under these conditions, mistakes were avoided, weaknesses were spotted early, differences were settled amicably, and the new products they introduced did significantly better in the marketplace.[4]

As an interesting contrast, Menon also found that conflict was destructive when managers distorted or withheld information, expressed hostility toward other ideas, or overstated their case to influence others.[5] When destructive conflict existed, mistakes were likely to go unnoticed, differences escalated into feuds, and new products were more likely to fare poorly in the marketplace.

Based on Menon's study and similar research, family businesses are more likely to promote constructive disagreement when they:

1. adhere to the suggestions in the preceding section on how to avoid groupthink;
2. adhere to a Code of Conduct that encourages civil conversations;
3. ensure that family members and other decision makers have sufficient information to process decisions;
4. provide family members with the opportunity to work closely together on some project to get to know, like, and trust each other;
5. ensure that roles are clear, particularly if there are overlapping areas of responsibility; and
6. ensure that authority, procedures, and resources to carry out tasks are sufficient and clear.

While families should realize much more constructive discussions by following the foregoing suggestions, it is wise to assume that there will still be occasions when differences of opinion are not easily resolved and disagreement deteriorates into conflict. In such instances, families need to be able to resolve that conflict quickly and successfully and prevent conflict from escalating. As unresolved conflict escalates, the tragic consequences can include business failure and sometimes permanent family divisions.

There are many popular methods of seeking to handle difficult conversations constructively. One of my favorite methods is known by the acronym "FAVES," which encourages participants to:

Focus (pay attention);
Ask questions;
Validate: acknowledge the emotions the other party is feeling;
Empathize: show that you understand how the other person feels; and
Summarize: reflect your understanding of what the other person said.[6]

Readers are encouraged to consider the numerous resources available on effective communication strategies.

A Case Study in Constructive Disagreement

I recently worked with a family business that was owned and managed by a father and son who were struggling to agree on whether to expand their business operations outside the United States. The father considered expansion a great idea; the son thought it too risky.

I met with them in order to explore their respective positions with a goal of bringing enhanced clarity to the criteria they were using to support their positions. The father acknowledged that his decision was based on "gut instinct"—something that had worked well for him in the past—and his sense that the international market had a significant financial upside potential. The son then explained his view that an international expansion would be risky and distract their focus from their increasingly successful domestic operations. We spent some time analyzing both positions, finally deciding that the best way to proceed was to adjourn for a week in order to allow the father to come back and report what the costs would be for a limited international launch along with some additional data on the market opportunity. We met again a week later and the father was able to bring some useful information into the discussion. After further dialogue, they decided to proceed with a limited international launch, a decision which seems to be working well.

Discussing their decision at the end of our meeting, both the father and son expressed their satisfaction with the process, particularly emphasizing the importance of remaining open, avoiding criticizing each other, and listening carefully and respectfully to the ideas they both presented. They also agreed to meet on a monthly basis for the specific purpose of evaluating how the international initiative was working and whether they should maintain it, expand it, or close it down. Beyond resolving this particular conflict successfully, the process gave the father and son a new sense of confidence in their ability to work through disagreements. I have also worked with a father and son who disagreed for years on whether to shut down their international operations. The process could never move beyond a discussion based on "gut feel" and proved to be quite challenging.

Anger Management

The American Psychological Association describes anger as "an emotion characterized by antagonism toward someone or something you feel has deliberately done you wrong."[7] It is natural to get angry, whether in the milder form of resentment or, in its most intense form, hate. Anger can be reflected in many ways, ranging from verbal abuse to physical violence. Whatever its cause, anger can create intra-family conflict that, if not managed, becomes increasingly challenging to resolve.

While every family business is different, our ancestral brains follow a pattern of escalating emotions when we believe we are being treated unfairly. These emotions are manifested modestly at first, often resulting in a family member "fleeing" from the cause of anger by, for example, ignoring e-mails or failing to show up at meetings. Unmanaged anger can escalate into dirty looks, sarcasm, or even violence. Anger obviously gets in the way of a family business's ability to flourish. Rather than focusing on how to best develop new products, services, markets, or opportunities, family members without workable anger-management tools often find themselves distracted by their anger. The consequences are tragic and, as discussed in the beginning of this book, are often the root cause of the high statistical failure rates within family businesses.

Because of the biological relationships existing between family members, the causes of anger within a family business are more complicated than in nonfamily businesses and organizations. The past and present relationships between mothers, fathers, siblings, and cousins aren't left at the office door when they show up for work or leave at the end of a day. Instead, a lifetime of roles, perceptions, and old scores remain, often fueling conflict that can be incomprehensible to nonfamily members who aren't sensitive to such dynamics. That's why even petty matters can create a sense of unfairness or unreasonableness. If siblings or cousins believe that a family member has secured a leadership position (particularly if accompanied by a generous compensation package) simply because of membership in the family, they may believe the family member to be incompetent and are likely to react angrily to real or perceived failings. Sadly, it is not unusual for petty disagreements to result in all-out family warfare. I recently met with two siblings whose disagreements all seemed petty to me but who, nevertheless, found themselves physically fighting each other in the offices of their family business. As Marcus Aurelius observed more than two thousand years ago, "how much more grievous are the consequences of anger than the cause of it."

One well-known example of a family relationship that deteriorated is that of the Koch brothers of Koch Industries, four brothers who fought for years over their massive fortune. In a *New York Times* story, journalist Leslie Wayne notes that the brothers' jealousy began in their childhood and, left unresolved, followed them to adulthood, where they eventually wound up in a bitter lawsuit with over a billion dollars at stake.[8]

At the end of the day, it is not always easy for family members to get along. The suggestions in this book are all about how to make it easier to do so. While I have focused on such strategies as higher-order thinking, principle-based decisions, smart and effective governance, and other mechanisms, sometimes the solutions for anger within a family business involve traditional treatment for anger management in order to give family members the tools they need to more constructively manage their emotions and concerns. Such programs can provide immeasurable benefits by helping family members understand the nature and causes of anger, how to avoid or minimize triggers for anger, and how to manage anger when it does occur. Dr. Andrew Newberg and Mark Waldman wrote a fascinating book on the intersection of neuroscience, communication, cooperation, and trust titled *Words Can Change Your Brain*. They observe that:

> [A]lthough we are born with the gift of language, research shows that we are surprisingly unskilled when it comes to communicating with others. We often choose our words without thought, oblivious of the emotional effects they can have on others. We talk more than we need to. We listen poorly, without realizing it, and we often fail to pay attention to the subtle meanings conveyed by facial expressions, body gestures, and the tone and cadence of our voice—elements of communication that are often more important than the words we actually say.[9]

Newberg and Waldman identify the following 12 strategies of "compassionate communication" demonstrated to enhance the quality of any conversation:

1. Relax
2. Stay present
3. Cultivate inner silence
4. Increase positivity
5. Reflect on your deepest values
6. Access a pleasant memory
7. Observe nonverbal cues
8. Express appreciation
9. Speak warmly
10. Speak slowly
11. Speak briefly
12. Listen deeply[10]

If a family can create a culture that allows issues to be avoided or managed in a respectful and thoughtful manner before they become problems, they will dramatically enhance the likelihood of a business succeeding.

One of the most valuable lessons family members can learn is that how they begin a difficult discussion can have a huge impact on whether the conversation goes well or goes poorly. Starting a difficult conversation in a positive and constructive manner can make all the difference. Strategies for doing so might include learning how to identify and check irrational thoughts and hidden agendas as well as learning to think strategically rather than emotionally.

A variety of tools and techniques are typically used when conflict arises within a family business. Some of these, such as mediation, arbitration, and litigation, are well known to lawyers. The next section considers some strategies that may be less well known to lawyers but that I have found very helpful over the years.

The Evolutionary Basis of Conflict Resolution

The history of life on earth is, in many respects, the history of repeated instances of cooperative behavior. The world can be a dangerous place for anything living, and survival has depended on mutual assistance and cooperation.

The universality of danger throughout the animal kingdom—and corresponding cooperative behavioral mechanisms among multiple animal species to guard against such danger—has been studied by numerous scientists, including Dr. Frans B.M. de Waal, Ph.D. Dr. de Waal wrote an interesting article titled *Primates—A Natural Heritage of Conflict Resolution*, exploring the subject of how nonhuman primates addressed and resolved disruptive conflict so they could get back to a more adaptive state of cooperation. The conclusions from such studies have important implications for resolving conflict within a family business.

Dr. de Waal observed that reconciling conflict "ensures the continuation of cooperation among parties . . ." adding that "[i]n many social animals . . . both parties stand to lose if escalated fighting damages relationships."[11] For this reason, it seems that nonhuman primates value social relationships, and the deterioration of those relationships must be prevented or resolved when it does occur.

Ongoing research of how humans make up after fighting suggests that mechanisms of cooperation exist not only across cultures but are quite similar in nature to how nonhumans resolve conflicts. While the study of cooperation through natural selection remains a core subject of interest in biology and related disciplines, de Waal suggests at least four mechanisms that can provide new or complementary tools to managing intra-family conflict:

1. Focus on the way conflict is handled and resolved.
2. Understand and respect the role of elders.
3. Take concrete actions to promote conciliation and forgiveness (e.g., getting together for a meal or drink).
4. Make compensatory payments (e.g., P/E Max).[12]

Two of these mechanisms, forgiveness and P/E Max, have been previously considered in chapters 3 and 6, respectively. The way in which conflict is handled and the role of elders are discussed below.

How Conflict Is Handled (A Brief Introduction to Game Theory)

While there are numerous ways to explore how conflict can be resolved, one of the most valuable planning tools that heretofore has received little attention in the family business literature is based on modern game theory. The power of applied game theory is actually suggested by the case study I describe later in this chapter, on page 144, involving two brothers who learned why they would be better off cooperating with each other rather than fighting.

Recognizing that the term "game theory" can sound intimidating, I'd like to begin by noting that game theory can be both easily understood and applied. Its insights have been used in a variety of everyday situations, whether related to business (such as in considering negotiation strategies related to collective bargaining or mergers and acquisitions agreements) or unrelated to business (such as in developing strategies for diplomacy and war, ethics, or politics). As Ken Binmore, professor emeritus of Economics at University College, London, notes:

> Drivers maneuvering in heavy traffic are playing a driving game. Bargain-hunters bidding on eBay are playing an auctioning game. A firm and a union negotiating next year's wage are playing a bargaining game. When opposing candidates choose their platform in an election, they are playing a political game. The owner of a grocery store deciding today's price for corn flakes is playing an economic game. In brief, a game is being played whenever human beings interact.[13]

So, what is game theory and how can it be used to benefit family businesses in conflict?

Alvin E. Roth of Harvard and Lloyd Shapley of UCLA won the 2012 Nobel Prize in economics for their work in finding the most efficient way to match parties in a transaction. Shapley used game theory to study matching models, which Roth built on to make real-world changes to existing markets, such as matching students to schools and organ donors to recipients.

Game theory typically begins with a "zero-sum game" involving two players. If one player wins, the other player loses. However, there are many varieties of games that are now studied, including games with multiple players and "positive-sum games," where all players may gain because of the exchanges between people. The classic game studied by theorists is known as the "Prisoner's Dilemma," in which two players are hypothetical partners in crime and have been captured by the police. The players are separated and offered an opportunity to confess in exchange for a reduced sentence. The choices facing the two players are as follows:

1. If Player A confesses and Player B does not, A goes free, testifies against B, and B goes to prison for three years.
2. If Player B confesses and Player A does not, B goes free and testifies against A, and A goes to prison for three years.

3. If both A and B confess, then both are convicted but given a reduced term of two years.
4. If neither player confesses, both are charged with a lesser offense and serve a term of one year.

The game is repeated a number of times, with each player forced to separately decide whether to "cooperate" with the other player (by admitting nothing) or to "defect" (in the hope of getting a lighter sentence). After each game, the players learn what the other player decided and are able to adjust their strategy for the following games. The winner is the player who serves the fewest number of years after all the games have been played.

Using a sample of data generated from many games, Robert M. Axelrod, a recognized authority on game theory, was able to prove that in the long run "altruistic players" tended to score better than "self-serving players." Self-serving players who confessed in the hope of being set free might win a game or two but their adversarial behavior is soon recognized and they are "punished" by the other player. In analyzing the top-scorers, Axelrod articulated the following conditions necessary for a strategy to be successful:

1. Good players start by cooperating, not defecting (or cheating).
2. If another player cheats, it can be important to retaliate so as not to be exploited.
3. Good players forgive defectors and start cooperating again—after retaliating—so as to prevent an ongoing negative spiral of defecting.
4. Good players seek to enhance their total score, not to score more than their opponent.[14]

While it might seem self-evident that an individual player should always confess—because he could go free if the player in the other cell does not confess—that behavior results in both players combined serving more years than if neither confessed. This conflict between the pursuit of individual goals and the common good is at the heart of many problems encountered within a typical family business because family members, like the "players" in a game, can be certain to interact with each other many times, adapting and responding to self-serving tendencies.

In many respects, family businesses would seem to offer the ideal environment for cooperation to emerge. Unfortunately, I suspect that many family members, driven by their ancestral brain, tend to react emotionally and fail to consider the consequences of misbehaving. When forced to think appreciatively and about what they accomplish as a team, it becomes easier to recognize the advantages of cooperating.

Game theory models like the prisoners' dilemma highlight the natural tension between cooperation and noncooperation. For a variety of reasons, including the ability of one player to punish another player for defecting, parties recognize the positive payoff for cooperating. So, while one might expect there to be more defecting (noncooperating) than cooperating, there is a clear bias toward cooperating. Common sense suggests that if we're generous to someone, that person is more likely to be generous toward us because people tend to reciprocate. Similarly, if we take advantage of another person, it wouldn't be surprising for that person to reciprocate by trying to take advantage of us or, at a minimum, to stop engaging with us. Family members would be wise to keep these basic principles in mind when interacting.

Using Game Theory to Resolve Conflict—A Case Study

Some time ago, two brothers came to my office where they proceeded to tell me that they owned several successful businesses together as 50-50 owners. Unfortunately, their relationship was so bad that they wanted to retain my legal services to help them go their separate ways. When I asked them how bad their relationship was, thinking that there might, perhaps, be an opportunity to use some of the strategies and techniques described in previous chapters, they told me that their fights weren't "only" verbal but physical as well and they had no interest in seeking to resolve their differences.

Continuing our discussion, I asked them what they had in mind for separating—whether each brother would get certain companies, or whether they would sell the businesses to a third party, or whether they had yet another option in mind. Not surprisingly, they hadn't thought about how to separate. Hearing that, I took out a piece of paper and started to list potential options that included, at one extreme, an immediate auction of company assets, presumably for pennies on the dollar, or, at the other extreme, continuing to run the businesses for some indeterminate amount of time to build value and then sell to a third party.

After a brief discussion, the brothers agreed that selling their assets at auction would be a terrible decision, as that would require them to leave millions of dollars of upside opportunity on the table. That decision, in turn, led me to my next question: in light of the unpleasant financial reality that would follow a decision to stop working together immediately, could they find a way not to hurt each other (literally) in the undefined "short term" while they worked to smartly position their business interests for sale? Having considered the options available to them, the brothers quickly concluded that they could work together.

The balance of our meeting was spent defining "rules of engagement" that the brothers agreed to live by from the time they left my office to the time they were able to separate in a more orderly fashion. Those rules were quite basic. For example, they agreed not to hit each other, to argue only in private, not to look backward into history in order to blame each other for current problems, and to work together to position their interests for sale as politely and civilly as possible.

While it remains to be seen how the brothers fare over the long haul, I can report at this time that several months have come and gone and I've had the chance to get together with them on occasion to catch up. While they are a long way from liking each other, they are no longer hurting each other and they seem to be finding a rhythm that is allowing them to cooperate to their mutual advantage.

> The January 2013 *ABA Journal* discusses how game theory is being increasingly applied to conflict resolution. One example discussed in the article is a program that has been developed by a law firm and a professor at NYU aimed at facilitating negotiations between business partners who would like to separate. The program requires each party to provide its confidential bid to acquire the company based on its view of value. The highest bidder will be the buyer—but the price is set at the average of the two values, thus allowing both parties to do better than their offer. Such programs have interesting potential application for helping family businesses resolve conflicts, including when a buyout becomes appropriate.[15]

Family Elders

As discussed in prior chapters, it can be very challenging to prevent our emotions from distorting our judgment when we're upset and angry. As a result, making smart decisions can be challenging. One common solution is to get a nonbiased perspective. Because of the often private and sensitive nature of the issues that give rise to conflict within a family business, a great third-party resource can be a senior family member (often referred to as an "elder") who, having the benefit of a longer lifetime of experiences, can offer a helpful perspective and advice.

Elders can often be extraordinarily helpful in resolving intra-family conflict and are often able to process information with perspective and good judgment. Helping family members distinguish the petty from the significant, they may be better able to identify a conciliatory path forward.

As discussed in the previous chapter, disputes that can't be resolved directly or through the help of an elder might also be brought to the family council or the board of directors to seek their assistance.

Professional Mediation

If, and only if, all options to resolve a dispute—either directly between the principals involved or with the assistance of a family elder, the family council, and the board of directors/advisers—have been unsuccessful, another option for families to consider is seeking the help of an outside mediator. Among other things, professional mediators are trained to be discreet and they know how to maintain their clients' confidences. Since mediation is completely voluntary, the family has the flexibility to agree to whatever rules of procedure they believe make sense under the circumstances. However, a typical mediation is characterized by the following core characteristics:

- the mediation is nonbinding on the parties;
- the mediator might meet, at times, privately with the parties in dispute and, at other times, with both parties present;
- good mediators are trained to help identify both legal and practical considerations so that: (1) the parties can consider both short- and long-term ramifications of their positions; and (2) each party better understands the other party's interests; and
- any settlement between the parties is voluntary.

Mediating family disputes can be quite challenging. The nature of the dispute may be significant enough that other conflict resolution mechanisms have proved unsuccessful because the nature of the conflict may have historical roots that date back many years. Understanding and working through the multiple levels of intra-family conflict can be challenging for any outsider to simply understand, much less solve, in the brief time frame allocated to mediations.

Accordingly, it is typically important for the mediator to meet with the parties as well as family leaders and outside professional advisers to better appreciate the personalities involved, the issues underlying the dispute, the options available, and other relevant considerations. These early conversations can also help clarify the "ground rules" for the mediation as well as establish trust and rapport in the mediator. Good family business mediators are not only skilled in the art of mediation, they are particularly sensitive to the nature of family businesses. They understand the complex roles and relationships involved and the importance of helping family members not just to resolve a particular dispute but to help them recognize their shared interests and minimize the possibility of ongoing disputes in the future. In many respects, the mediator's job is to help family members recognize the trade-off between the consequences of failing to resolve their dispute (lose-lose) and the consequences of finding a constructive and acceptable path forward (win-win).

Collaborative Law

The field of collaborative law represents a promising new way in which lawyers are seeking to use their training, experience, and creativity to help their clients resolve disputes. Having its origins in family law, collaborative law is a form of dispute resolution that seeks to emphasize finding solutions rather than finding fault. Consistent with the underlying premises of positive psychology, the collaborative process is designed to minimize, if not eliminate, negative emotions such as anger, resentment, and frustration that often accompany an adversarial approach when seeking to resolve disputes in a traditional fashion.

While I am not aware of an instance in which collaborative law has been used to help resolve family business disputes, its potential application for such a purpose seems both obvious and promising. The process and its benefits are explored below.

The Collaborative Process

Collaborative lawyers generally begin by introducing the process to their clients, including its philosophy, its ground rules, and its potential advantages and disadvantages over alternative dispute resolution mechanisms. Typically, the collaborative process is structured so that each party retains his or her own lawyer, both of whom agree to withdraw from their respective representations if the dispute isn't settled and the parties decide to litigate the matter. The logic of such a requirement is to help structurally guarantee that the parties' interests are fully aligned toward achieving a successful outcome through negotiated settlement instead of prolonged litigation. Sensitive to the challenges in communication highlighted in chapter 5, the parties commonly agree that all discussions will be conducted through face-to-face meetings, not through letters, e-mails, or telephone calls.

After meeting privately with their respective lawyers to discuss the process, the parties and their lawyers have what is typically referred to as a "four-way meeting" to ensure that the parties are committed to working out an agreement without going to court and then memorializing that agreement in a signed document. The parties share their main goals and objectives and agree on how to move forward to address the parties' concerns and help them reach an agreement. Assuming they are successful, the parties confirm their agreement in writing, including by specifying what, if anything, needs to be done in order to implement the agreement. Because of the private nature of the collaborative process, there are no court-imposed deadlines, which allows the process to be scheduled around the parties' interests and convenience.

Benefits of Collaborative Law

Collaborative practice may offer several advantages over more traditional forms of dispute resolution, like arbitration and mediation, and these advantages should be considered in the event of an intra-family conflict. For example, binding arbitration leaves the ultimate resolution of a dispute in the hands of an arbitrator rather than the family members. Further, while mediation leaves decision making in the family's hands, the process is guided by a mediator whose knowledge about the underlying facts and circumstances that generated the conflict may be quite limited. Collaborative law seems to offer a number of benefits, including a process that (1) seeks to move the parties to higher-order thinking through engagement in problem-solving or possibility-seeking conversations rather than fighting; (2) forgiveness through apologies, if appropriate, is encouraged; and (3) the professionals are motivated to resolve a dispute by agreeing to disengage if the parties can't find a resolution and decide to pursue litigation. The following statistical data cited by Wray and Clemmensen suggest that these and related factors have proven quite successful:

> Of the cases reported by clients, 90% settled in the collaborative process and 10% terminated prior to settlement of all issues. 75% of clients reported being satisfied with Collaborative Practice overall, with 39% being extremely satisfied and 36% being somewhat satisfied.
>
> ... For the 90% of clients whose cases settled in the Collaborative process, the overall rating was higher. 79% of clients whose cases settled reported being satisfied, with 43% being extremely satisfied and 36% being somewhat satisfied.[16]

Because the failure rate of family businesses remains high, professional advisers can't complacently continue to rely on only the traditional dispute resolution mechanisms of mediation, arbitration, and litigation. Consideration should also be given to innovative alternative dispute resolution approaches when family conflict erupts, including retaining settlement counsel to complement the efforts of litigation counsel, as they will focus on settlement strategy rather than litigation strategy.

Selling the Company or Buying Out Family Members

While I accept the practical reality that litigation will remain a dispute resolution option for families locked in conflict, I am convinced that it is a terrible option for family matters. It is an option where even the nominal winner is a loser, as that party has spent money on professional fees and expenses and has been distracted by the time and energy the litigation process demands, and, perhaps most importantly of all, litigation renders authentic reconciliation virtually impossible because of the adversarial nature of litigation. Win or lose, the parties stand very little hope of rebuilding genuine trust in each other and again working together successfully—much less come together as a united and loving family.

Accordingly, my conflict resolution recommendation of last resort—offered only in the event that all other options highlighted in this chapter fail to work—is for one or more family members to sell their interests to other family members or, alternatively, for the entire family to sell its interests to an outside third party. The selling family members will have cash in exchange for their illiquid ownership interest in the business that they can use to support their lifestyle or, if they are entrepreneurial, can use to seed a new business venture.

> It is not unusual for family members who are prepared to sell their interests in the business to be reluctant to do so out of concern (fear) that they would be selling too cheaply and the acquiring family members might take advantage of them. To help manage that fear, I have found it useful to include a formulaic adjustment to the selling price that would provide the selling family member with additional consideration if the family member who is buying that ownership interest, in turn, sells the business at a premium price compared to what the original selling family member sold at. For example, if two siblings own a business equally, and one sells the business for $1 million—i.e., a $2 million valuation—and the sibling buying the business turns around the very next day and sells the entire company for $10 million, the original seller could logically conclude that he unfairly lost $4 million dollars in the process because, had they sold together, he would have realized $5 million in the transaction. A provision sometimes referred to as a "look-back adjustment" can provide comfort that the seller would share in the "premium" realized from a follow-on sale—typically based on a sliding scale that might start by sharing 100 percent of the premium for a short period of time, then ratchet gradually down over a period of three to five years, say from 80 percent to 60 percent to 40 percent, ultimately terminating so that the proceeds realized from a sale beyond the expiration of the look-back period would no longer be shared.

Conclusion

There is no bright-line test that distinguishes constructive disagreement from counterproductive conflict. Indeed, because we are all unique, what one individual might experience as conflict, another might experience as a robust discussion.

Because of this reality and because the circumstances that give rise to conflict are often unique, there is no "one size fits all" approach to conflict preemption and resolution. Ideally, the individuals involved in the conflict need to be sensitive to the existence of developing disagreement and seek to resolve their differences before the issues get out of hand. If other stakeholders are sensitive to a developing disagreement, they might seek to constructively intervene before the disagreement ripens into a more serious conflict. In circumstances where such informal dispute resolution mechanisms are unsuccessful, family businesses would be well served by having a clear approach to seeking to resolve conflict, often drawing on a variety of mechanisms that, with increasing formality, might be helpful. The key to resolving these differences constructively is often a function of how actively the parties are listening, and how authentically they seek to process differences in opinions and ensure that differences are resolved without ever rising to the level of a destructive conflict. Constructive disagreement generally seems to occur when individuals seek to understand and appreciate the various viewpoints of others involved in the conversation and discuss and resolve their differences of opinion while avoiding negative behavior that could escalate the situation into disruptive conflict.

The impact on intra-family trust resulting from a change in focus from conflict resolution to conflict preemption is reflected in Figure 13.

Figure 13: The Impact of Success Factor 6—Conflict Preemption

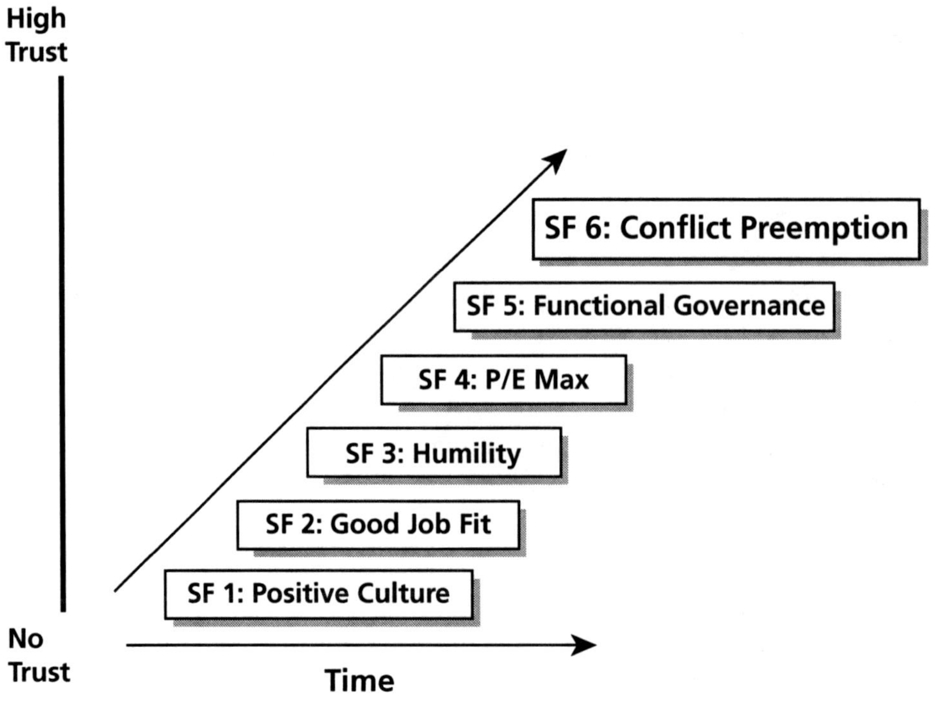

Quotations

"Wise men do not quarrel with each other."

Danish proverb

"There was never a good war or a bad peace."

Benjamin Franklin

"Deep-seated preferences cannot be argued about."

Oliver Wendell Holmes, Jr.

"It is much easier to avoid disagreement than to remove discontents."

George Washington

Next Generation Planning 9

"Before beginning, plan carefully."

Cicero

Background: Failure Factor 7 (Technically Designed Plans That Ignore Family Dynamics)

Like all businesses, family businesses typically spend a lot of time and money planning. Most family businesses engage professional advisers to help them prepare estate and retirement plans; many also engage advisers to help prepare compensation, strategic, and other plans. Increasingly, more families engage advisers to assist in the preparation of succession plans. I have no doubt that most of these plans are technically superb and, at least theoretically, get the job done.

However, the problem with traditional family business planning initiatives is that "reasonable people" don't always exist in a family business where stakeholders, often driven by fear, are more likely to behave unreasonably. I'm pretty confident that any professional who regularly works with family businesses might think the notion of a "reasonable family business member" is something of an oxymoron. As a result, many "theoretically great plans" simply don't work as planned because family businesses are fueled by people's emotions, feelings, and instincts, not just by data, numbers, and statistics.

Failure Factor 7 characterizes the challenges family businesses face when their planning ignores real-world emotional and psychological considerations. In many respects, this failure factor underlies the entire premise of this book: that professional advisers need to expand their planning paradigm and skill set, directly or in collaboration with other professionals, so that they can help their clients engage in a more holistic planning process. Because there are countless strategies to apply the exciting work that has taken place in the field of positive psychology, the balance of this chapter seeks to suggest some of the ways in which these insights can be applied to complement and improve the traditional plans that a family business needs.

Parental Planning—Raising Children

When family business owners and their advisers focus on wealth management plans, they seem to spend a disproportionate amount of time thinking about how that wealth can be used to fund senior family members' retirements or how to reduce estate and gift taxes. Little time seems to be spent on parenting responsibilities and challenges that accompany raising children who are born into a family that owns a business, many of which create a level of financial success that can be detrimental to the healthy development of children if care isn't taken. This phenomenon is sometimes referred to as "affluenza," reflecting the failure of children to live up to their potential because they were spoiled by money.

A number of great resources can be consulted on how children can be parented to enhance the likelihood that they will flourish as they mature and remain cohesive members of the family. Common suggestions include the following:

1. Ensure that the family spends time together (whether at the dinner table or at a school activity) and takes part in family get-togethers on a regular basis. Spending time together is a great way to transmit core values.
2. Understand that parents are role models for their children, and as such they should model behaviors they'd like to see in their children, such as hard work, respect for other people, respect for the value of a dollar, etc.
3. Discuss social initiatives that are of interest to the family, including charitable work and philanthropy—and encourage children to get involved in supporting a community initiative of interest.
4. Encourage children to discover their own interests, whether they relate to the family's existing business interests or not.
5. Encourage children to get a job outside of the family business to help broaden their perspective.

"Tell me and I forget, teach me and I may remember, involve me and I learn."

Benjamin Franklin

Compensation and Benefits Plans

H.L. Mencken wryly observed that wealth is "any income that is at least one hundred dollars more a year than the income of one's wife's sister's husband." The public conflict of wealthy families such as the Pritzkers and Latners suggests Mencken's remark was not just funny, but insightful, and that any family might be at risk if family members don't understand and support the allocation of the wealth their business creates.

Many family businesses traditionally compensate family members of the same generation at equal rates of pay in order to "keep things fair." The equal pay concept usually results from a parental instinct to treat all children the same. One problem with such an approach is that job responsibilities are rarely the same and treating family members equally doesn't mean that they are being treated equitably. On the other hand, by making distinctions in compensation, family members are apt to feel (when on the low side of the equation) that the distinctions are without merit and unfair. A sense of unfairness may be an inevitable result when family members work together. For reasons previously considered, unhappy family members will lose focus on the business, instead bringing negative focus on money in the form of jealousy and resentment. Ultimately, talented family members might choose to work elsewhere or, if not, tension will continue to escalate and likely turn to conflict.

Accordingly, one of the biggest imperatives and challenges for any business is to compensate employees effectively. Successful family business owners recognize the need to compensate their employees, including family employees, in a manner that creates incentives for excellent performance and fosters a positive culture where individual goals are aligned with team goals. Companies that are able to recognize and reward good performances are better positioned to attract and retain talented workers; companies that fail to do so will likely have unmotivated workers and may risk losing their family employees to better-managed organizations.

Compensation planning can be complex and challenging. A thoughtfully prepared plan needs to be tailored to support a particular business's unique structure and objectives. Attesting to the complexity of the planning process, an entire industry has been built to offer advice on how to create effective compensation plans.

Because of the business and family dynamics, compensation planning within a family business can be particularly tricky. Not only must the traditional purposes of the plan be served (such as incentivizing an employee to focus on sales, or quality, or something else of importance to the family business), but the plan must also foster understanding and supportive intra-family relationships. Otherwise, driven by the ancestral, fear-based part of their brains, family employees are apt to:

- fear they aren't getting paid enough compared to other family employees and/or owners;
- fear they aren't being appropriately recognized, whether with promotions, bonuses, or awards; or
- fear they aren't receiving the same amount or quality of perks and other benefits that other family members receive.

In short, creating a smart and principled compensation plan is one of the most critical requirements to ensuring that talented family members remain motivated, loyal, and hardworking contributors to the success of a family business.

In the November 2012 *ABA Journal*, Brian Sullivan shared this story about how compensation disputes within a family business can put a damper on holiday feasts:

Frosty dinner conversation is all but guaranteed for Salvatore and Patricia Piazza, who own Piazza's Ice Cream & Ice House, a distribution business on Staten Island. They made their son, Nicholas, the company's vice president. Nicholas, dissatisfied with what he considered low pay and long hours, complained to his parents and claims he was fired as a result. He then bought a truck and allegedly began to lure customers away from his parents' business. They sued him in May, seeking a permanent injunction and $500,000 in damages.

Nicholas answered with a lawsuit of his own in July, claiming that he was illegally denied overtime pay and demanding $100,000 in damages.[2]

Essential Elements of a Basic Compensation Plan

I have found that the problem with many family businesses is that they don't have a plan. Without a compensation plan, families tend to make ad hoc and inconsistent decisions, sometimes trying to treat all family members equally, sometimes disproportionately rewarding family members who work in the business. The lack of clarity and consistency is the root of many problems. For the reasons discussed in chapter 6, family businesses would be wise to construct a principled and consistently applied compensation plan designed to motivate employees to work in support of the organization's core principles, including its values, mission, vision, and policies. Such a plan should be in writing and should also define performance measures and benchmarks to ensure that family members understand how they will be compensated as employees—whether by some objective formula, by subjective criteria, or by some combination of objective and subjective criteria.

Because there are often opportunities to benefit family members through more than just salaries, a plan might further specify:

- whether salaries are based on the responsibility and contribution an individual makes to a business, and are consistent with market rates or are based on family status. Market-rate compensation plans are inherently more equitable and more likely to be successful in satisfying family members with passive ownership interests who don't draw salaries for working in the business.
- whether and how incentive bonuses, based on meeting or exceeding personal, team, or company goals and accomplishments, are to be awarded.
- the number of available vacation and sick days, retirement benefits, health benefits, tuition reimbursement, and other fringe benefits.
- the type of perks available to family members and the basis on which they are awarded.

Whatever compensation plan a family may decide is most appropriate for its circumstances, it is important that the plan be communicated to family stakeholders so that they understand how it works and whether it works for them. A family member who finds the plan irrational or unfair is always free to work elsewhere.

> Dividends or distributions, depending on the legal form of the family business, can be made to owners of a family business based on the company's profits, regardless of whether an owner works in the business and receives a salary. Dividends, which are mathematically calculated, can be a useful way to provide all family members with some economic benefits simply because they are members of the family, whether they work in the family business or not.

Retirement Planning

Retirement is traditionally understood as an event that marks the end of one's working life. Many working people look forward to retiring so that they can permanently relax by getting out of the rat race. There is no shortage of advice on how to plan for retirement. The professionals providing retirement planning advice have traditionally focused on the need to save and invest money wisely in anticipation of the time when their clients won't be earning an income. They focus on such initiatives as setting goals, choosing investment options, and considering tax planning.

> Within a family business, the retirement process is often juxtaposed with the succession planning process, since the retirement of a family leader requires that someone else succeed him or her unless the business is sold or shut down. Succession planning considerations are discussed below.

A problem with many retirement planning initiatives is that little or no attention may be given to equally important psychological considerations that can naturally result when the prospective retiree worries about no longer feeling productive and engaged through work. Fearing the loss of stature, purpose, and income, many family members hang on to their positions within their company for as long as they possibly can, often choosing not to retire at all. Indeed, a recent study conducted by Arthur Andersen's American Family Business Survey found that between one-quarter and one-third of leaders of family businesses either don't intend to retire or plan to remain involved in some capacity throughout their lives.[3]

One of the most interesting developments in the field of retirement planning involves a new focus on initiatives designed to promote healthy and enjoyable retirement experiences. One of the more prominent efforts is Stanford University's Center on Longevity (http://longevity.stanford.edu/) that explores through scientific research how to enhance the retirement experience. George Vaillant, a professor at Harvard Medical School, charted the lives of hundreds of men and women over decades. He identified seven factors that predict "positive aging": (1) not smoking or quitting smoking while still young; (2) mature coping styles (turning lemons into lemonade); (3) absence of alcohol abuse; (4) healthy weight; (5) stable marriage; (6) exercise; and (7) years of education. In Vaillant's words, "the mission of positive aging is very clear; to add more life to years, not just more years to life."[4]

Attention to how to enhance the retirement experience, particularly in light of longer life expectancies, demands changes in our approach to aging and retirement planning. If we continue to limit our planning to financial issues, families in business together will continue to struggle with how to accommodate new generations of family members vying for opportunities to exercise leadership that senior members are reluctant to give up.

Joan Carter, cofounder of Life Options Institute, offers the following retirement tips:

1. **Retirement living is about more than money.** Financial planners tell us to start thinking about retirement living decades before we're ready to retire, and it's good to make a retirement planning checklist about five years before your retirement date. While you're thinking about how much money you'll need in retirement, think about what you want your life to look like, and how you want to feel.

2. **Make life plans.** It's important to plan for the nonfinancial aspect of retirement living by considering what will make you happy. . . . Make a life plan and tick off your experiences as you move ahead. And no, I'm not talking about a 'Bucket list.'

3. **Find a purpose.** When making your retirement living plan, look for things you can do on an ongoing basis that bring you joy and add structure to your life. These can include travel, hobbies, or even training for a new career.

4. **Keep your mind sharp.** "Use it or lose it" applies to your brain. If you feel the need to replace the intellectual stimulation you found at work, try learning a foreign language or a musical instrument, or join a book club. Lifelong learning offers many opportunities to keep your mind sharp . . .

5. **Volunteer.** Getting involved in your community is a great way to give back, and it's a wonderful opportunity to interact with people and make new friends . . .

6. **Develop new friendships.** Check out groups that help you meet new people or join community or religious organizations that have members who share your interests . . . It's possible to meet people and make new friends even if it's difficult to get around. Friendship helps to increase longevity.

7. **Ask your spouse or partner.** If you live with someone or have a close partner, retirement living becomes a shared experience. It's important to make time for you and your partner to both share your dreams. . . .

8. **Increase your financial stability.** If you can't afford to retire yet, consider partial retirement. This can include working part-time in your current job or finding a retirement job that's new and interesting—and will help you earn money.

(continued)

9. **Keep your spirits up.** The life changes that come with retirement can be challenging, but your attitude plays a big part in whether you'll find happiness or not. . . . Learn the signs of senior depression, ask a friend or family member to assess your mood, and don't be afraid to ask for help.

10. **Remain healthy.** . . . With increasing life spans, retirement living can be a long race, so get yourself in shape. That means eating well, watching your weight, and staying active. When you feel good, it's easier to stay positive and open to new experiences.[5]

Estate Planning

I recall working with a family business that underwent an ownership and management transition when the company founder died unexpectedly. The father, whose three children worked in the business, had ruled with an iron fist. In spite of being very smart, he had failed to spend much time on his estate plan and had not discussed the subject with his children. His unexpected death left the family unprepared for a smooth succession of business leadership.

The man's widow, who inherited majority ownership of the business, did her best to keep peace in the family, but the children bickered. The only son, who already had a strong leadership role in the business, convinced his mother to give him even more responsibility.

The son soon had virtually unlimited authority to run the family business. The daughters felt that their father's intentions were being violated and that leadership of the family business should have been shared equally by all three siblings. The daughters accused their mother of favoring her son. Ultimately, the family business broke apart and the daughters left to start their own company.

The father's silence on leadership succession in this family business contributed to his children battling to advance their own self-interest, ultimately resulting in his family splintering.

Such disasters occur every day in family businesses around the world. Sometimes, the leader's intentions were clear but never communicated to his survivors. Other times, the leader simply ignored the difficult planning decisions that inevitably arise. In either case, the surviving family members are left with little guidance on how to lead the company.

Much like retirement planning, traditional work around estate planning is focused on the disposition of material assets in an orderly and tax-efficient fashion. This narrowly focused approach has contributed to many unfortunate family disputes over the years that could be avoided through a more holistic approach to estate planning. I have worked with family businesses over the years where the leader, in spite of my advice, elected to avoid the perhaps difficult responsibility of explaining the logic of his or her decisions to family members prior to passing away. The results have often been unfortunate and I have seen family relationships implode, with siblings suing siblings and businesses unraveling. Without the benefit of helpful guidance, I have seen children argue about what their parents "really meant" in their will, or how they would have wanted a particular situation handled. The discussions tend to start off congenially but often disintegrate into bickering, where individuals are prone to think of themselves less as siblings and more as beneficiaries, seeking to promote their own self-interest.

While it would seem to be possible to proactively address these issues while a parent is still alive, the estate planning process is a generally unpleasant experience because individuals are forced to contemplate the finiteness of their lives.[6]

Notwithstanding this unpleasantness, professionals can help their clients focus on certain positive psychological aspects of preparing an estate plan. One obvious benefit, of course, is in helping clients appreciate the sense of accomplishment that can come from having a desired testamentary plan made, memorialized, and distributed according to their wishes.[7] Another opportunity is to help clients move past the typically exclusive focus on the transmission of material assets by focusing on the transmission of intangible assets through an ethical will.

Ethical Wills

Although considerable thought often goes into the typical estate plan for a principal in a family business, many plans completely ignore sharing two critical items: (1) perspective and rationale as to why certain decisions were made, including why certain assets were transferred to designated beneficiaries; and (2) intangible assets, such as knowledge, insights, and advice. An ancient planning tool with roots in the Bible, known as an "ethical will," can help surviving family members in important ways.

An ethical will, which can be prepared in forms such as letters or videotapes, is intended to share important information that might not otherwise belong or easily fit into a will, trust, or other testamentary document. While there is no limit to the type of information that one might share, ethical wills can be particularly helpful to impart the logic and rationale behind decisions of leadership, succession, ownership, and governance. While a traditional estate plan might establish *how* the ownership interests in a family business will be transferred, an ethical will can be used to explain *why* those interests are being transferred in that way and any other relevant background information.

An ethical will can also be used to ensure the transmission of deeply held values and beliefs gleaned over the course of a lifetime. It can also be helpful to include suggestions and recommendations about professional advisers who family members might turn to in resolving certain matters. In short, an ethical will can be used to help create a lasting legacy of wisdom and insight that survivors might find helpful, personally and collectively.

> Paul Ciminelli, the CEO and owner of Ciminelli Development Company, a successful second-generation real estate development business headquartered in western New York, has written an ethical will. Ciminelli, who succeeded his father, Frank, in the business, wanted to share his core values with his two sons, Tory and Kyle. In his ethical will, Ciminelli explains why he made certain decisions (including why he decided to pursue a career in his family business), thoughts on how to achieve a healthy balance in life, and insights into his relationship with his father.
>
> Ciminelli makes it clear that his children need not feel obligated to join his business, but if they do, there are ground rules and prerequisites for doing so. He prepared his ethical will to help ensure that he successfully transfers his values, lessons, and insights—not just material wealth—to his children.

Preparation Tips

Because it is personal in nature and has no binding legal effect, there is no "right way" to prepare an ethical will. While traditionally an ethical will is shared upon the author's death, it might be more helpful to review and discuss the document with family members while the author is still alive. Giving family members an opportunity to ask questions may enhance the family's understanding about certain decisions the author has made during his lifetime as well as those that will take effect upon his death.

For the reasons discussed in chapter 5, individuals should consider recording an ethical will on CD or DVD to enhance nonverbal communication through facial expressions, emotions, and tone of voice. Ethical wills can, and perhaps should, be updated over the years to reflect changing circumstances and perspectives. Finally, it is important to remember that an ethical will is not a legally enforceable instrument and should be considered only a supplement to traditional estate planning instruments.

Creating an ethical will can be a positive experience for its author and can offer valuable and important insights to family members, helping ensure the memorialization of one's legacy.

Succession Planning

> "A successful business is often the best thing that can happen to a family—and the worst. There often seems to be nothing scientific about the management of a family company. Much of what goes on is rooted in emotion, and succession is the most emotional issue of all. Business professors hate this kind of situation; psychiatrists thrive on it. The biggest challenge in family businesses is the patriarch who lingers too long." Gordon Pitts—
> *In the Blood—Battles to Succeed in Canada's Family Businesses*[8]

Sheldon Gary Adelson, the chairman and chief executive officer of the Las Vegas Sands Corporation and other business interests, has been quoted as saying, "Why do I need succession planning? I'm very alert, I'm very vibrant. I have no intention to retire."[9] This sort of comment is not at all unusual and reminds me of a one-page marketing piece a friend of mine in the insurance business showed me many years ago that he used with his clients to prompt discussion about estate planning. The gist of the piece asks: "When do you expect to die: (a) in the next year? (b) in the next five years? (c) in the next 20 years? or (d) never?"

"Succession planning," a phrase commonly used to refer to the transition of leadership from one generation to the next, can be an extremely complicated and challenging process in a family business because it implicates a variety of subjects, including financial considerations, interpersonal relationships, and leadership readiness—both to step down by a current leader and to step up by a prospective leader. Any one of these subjects can be problematic to address on its own so when combined, succession planning tends to be very challenging and often requires a lot of time and attention. Indeed, the subject can be so overwhelming that it is often ignored, leaving family businesses to work through leadership transitions upon an individual's death in an ad hoc, unprincipled, and often unsatisfactory fashion.

Ivan Landsberg, a former professor at Yale and Columbia, an acclaimed author, and a preeminent family business consultant, cites a number of forces in his landmark book on succession planning, *Succeeding Generations*. Landsberg observes that the succession planning process can be particularly challenging due to founders, who often fear death and the loss of power and control; founder spouses, who often fear the loss of stature from changing roles within the business; and employees, who often fear the changes that might result from having a new boss, including prospective changes in interpersonal relationships as well as changes in job responsibilities and authorities.[10] Lansberg describes the importance of developing a culture of collaboration across family branches. "Collaboration," he writes, "depends on maintaining and strengthening the bonds of trust in the family."[11] He explains that:

> Trust is a complex phenomenon which has five major components—what I call the "five Cs." First, trust grows in families when the members have confidence in one another's *competence* . . . Second, trust is enhanced when a family member's behavior is *congruent*—in other words, when others can rely on the person to do what he or she says. Trust also depends on *consistent* behavior that is predictable and not erratic. . . . Another requirement of trust—"the fourth C"—is *compassion.* . . . The "fifth C"—*communication*—is the foundation on which trust is built.[12]

Overcoming family and individual fears can be challenging and, to be successful, requires the commitment of the family and employees of the business.

Because many great resources on the subject of succession planning can be consulted by professional advisers or family members who are unfamiliar with the process, I'll simply note that successful successions often share the following qualities:

1. They are more likely to take place over a period of time, resulting in a natural transition rather than an abrupt transition that takes place as an event on a particular and somewhat arbitrary day.
2. They generally include the clear articulation of relevant criteria, used in a committed fashion, in selecting a successor. "Relevant criteria" might include such factors as education, experience, emotional intelligence, etc. "Irrelevant criteria" might include sex, birth order, or expectations resulting from simply being a member of the family. Establishing and relying on relevant criteria can minimize stakeholder fears that a successor will be chosen on the basis of criteria largely unimportant to the needs of the business, which could put the family's investment at risk. Having nonfamily member directors involved in the selection process can help ensure that the selection process is based on rational and articulated criteria.
3. A successor continuously seeks to develop his or her leadership skills, even after assuming a leadership position.
4. Consistent with the discussion in chapter 4, children who choose to work in, and ultimately lead, the family business, are there because they are genuinely interested in and capable of doing so.
5. There is ongoing and robust communication among family members, including at family council meetings and family retreats, about the succession process. As a result of such communication, family members all understand the process that has been or will be developed, the criteria that will be used to select a successor, and how and when the plan will

be executed over time. Such meetings also provide family members with an opportunity to ask questions and raise concerns that, in turn, might be addressed as needed.

> For any number of reasons, including interests, technical capability, leadership skills, etc., the best successor might turn out to be a nonfamily member. Great family businesses recognize the important role that nonfamily members can have in leading a family business, and they find ways to allow both family and nonfamily members to work together. For example, Richemont, the family business that owns such famous brands as Cartier and Montblanc, recently announced that Johann Rupert would be stepping down as chief executive in 2013 and will be succeeded by two nonfamily members, Bernard Fornas, who will be responsible for overseeing Richemont's operating companies, including watchmaker Jaeger-LeCoultre and fashion house Chloe, and Richard Lepeu, who will run the family's central operations.[13]

The impact on intra-family trust resulting from a more holistic planning approach is reflected in Figure 14.

Figure 14: The Impact of Success Factor 7—Next Generation Planning

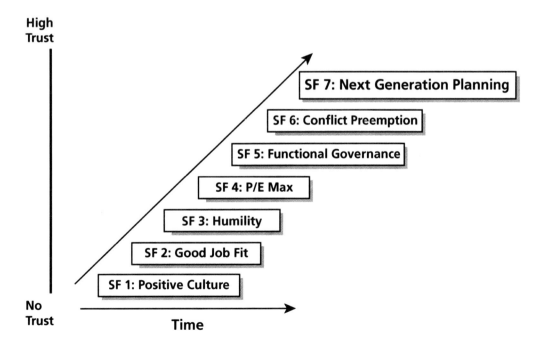

Quotations

"The only thing we know about the future is that it is going to be different."

Peter Drucker

"Don't cross the bridge until you come to it, and then be sure there is a bridge."

Anonymous

"Change is the law of life. And those who look only to the past or present are certain to miss the future."

President John F. Kennedy

Conclusion | 10

"Coming together is a beginning. Keeping together is progress. Working together is success."

Henry Ford

There are many benefits to family businesses, including the pride that comes from family members building a successful enterprise, the loyalty and support that family members can offer each other, job benefits that are often unusual such as flexible working hours, and the possibility of creating employment opportunities and wealth for future generations.

However, the statistical rate at which family businesses fail to transition from generation to generation highlights the many challenges that come with family businesses. While we are blessed by evolution, we are also at risk as a result of its by-products. As a species, we are fooled by randomness, we behave in predictably irrational ways, we hear but don't listen, our memories fail us, and, perhaps most problematic of all, we often react emotionally as a result of our ancestral brains continuing to process fear as if our lives were in jeopardy. Any one of these evolutionary consequences can create major challenges for families in business together; in the aggregate they represent a major threat to families who choose to work together and can easily result in damaging both family and business.

The suggestions in this book are intended to offer a new planning paradigm for family businesses and their professional advisers based on a better understanding of the challenges resulting from these evolutionary by-products and cognitive imperfections. Accompanying this new paradigm are tools and strategies to keep these challenges in check by explicitly planning to reinforce intra-family trust. My experience working with family businesses for almost three decades gives me great confidence that families can beat the high statistical rate of failure driven by the invisible yet natural forces I have referred to as failure factors. The suggestions set forth in this book, which, I refer to as success factors, serve as antidotes to these failure factors by helping families:

1. Move from a fear-based culture to a positive culture.
2. Move from filling jobs based on convenience to filling jobs based on good fit.
3. Recognize the challenges in communicating and foster a culture that values humility.
4. Become a P/E Max organization by clarifying and committing to core principles.
5. Professionalize governance with a board of directors and a family council.
6. Develop plans so that disagreements can be managed constructively and use new strategies to resolve conflict as early as possible.
7. Consider how traditional planning initiatives can benefit from the insights of positive psychology and neuroscience and help create the next generation of plans.

Each of these Seven Success Factors offers great benefits and, in combination, can reinforce trust and enhance the likelihood of families in business together succeeding and flourishing, from generation to generation. The impact on intra-family trust resulting from the application of these seven success factors is reflected in Figure 15.

Figure 15: Family Business Planning Strategies for the 21st Century

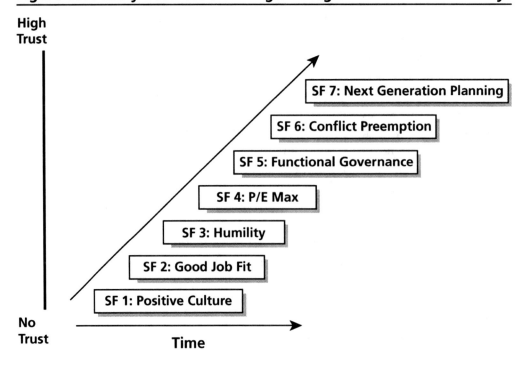

The Seven Success Factors can be deployed incrementally to most appropriately fit individual families' needs and circumstances. In contemplating "where to begin" in one's search for happiness, Bob Rich and I encouraged our readers in *Secrets from The Delphi Café* to consider "HOPE":

The secret is to focus on—

High impact
Opportunities (rather than problems). Always act from your
Principles (rather than expediency) and choose to work first on areas that are
Easy to resolve or put into effect so as to build momentum for ongoing initiatives.[1]

I have found the same approach works nicely for family businesses.

The legal profession's recognition of the need to apply insights from such fields as evolutionary biology, neuroscience, and positive psychology is beginning to take hold. The University of Wisconsin-Madison established an integrated dual-degree program in neuroscience and law in 2012 that offers students the opportunity to earn a Ph.D. in neuroscience and a J.D. in law; and Baylor College of Medicine has started a neuroscience and law initiative. In commenting on the relevance of neuroscience to criminal law, the director of the Baylor program, neuroscientist and best-selling author David Eagleman, noted that:

[t]he brain is an enormously complicated system, and there are a vast number of factors that influence who you are and how you behave . . . People become who they are from a complex interaction of their genes and all their experiences—from what happened in the womb, to the neighborhood you grow up in, to the culture in which you are embedded.[2]

These exciting programs suggest new opportunities to understand and better manage the many complex subjects that are regulated or served by the legal system. Given their enormous impact on the economy and the possibilities that exist to help individuals and their families flourish, it is high time to change the planning paradigm that now exists and incorporate these new tools and strategies suggested by science to better serve family businesses.

Recognizing that wealthy families still struggle to flourish, I developed the Family Business Scorecard some years ago to give families in business together a better sense of how they are performing without regard to

(continued)

traditional financial metrics and how well positioned they are for continuing their business over the generations. The scorecard is intended to give family business owners and stakeholders a better sense of their exposure to failure factors as well as how well they might be immunized by having focused on the success factors described in this book. The scorecard is reproduced in Appendix 1 and can be taken without charge online at www.lippes.com. I have used the scorecard to (1) provide an objective analysis of critical issues facing every family business; (2) determine the existence of "hot spots" to promote early intervention; (3) provide objective criteria to help make solid family and business decisions; and (4) map dynamic changes in family business health.

Quotation

"How long we shall continue to blunder along without the aid of unpartisan and authoritative scientific assistance in the administration of justice, no one knows; but all fair persons not conventionalized by provincial legal habits of mind ought, I should think, unite to effect some such advance."

Judge Learned Hand

Appendix 1
The Family Business Scorecard

1.	Family members in the business are there, in large measure, because they love what they do. ❏ Strongly Disagree ❏ Disagree ❏ Possible ❏ Agree ❏ Strongly Agree
2.	We have a clear statement of values. ❏ Strongly Disagree ❏ Disagree ❏ Possible ❏ Agree ❏ Strongly Agree
3.	Roles and responsibilities are clearly defined. ❏ Strongly Disagree ❏ Disagree ❏ Possible ❏ Agree ❏ Strongly Agree
4.	Family members meet regularly to receive updates on important matters. ❏ Strongly Disagree ❏ Disagree ❏ Possible ❏ Agree ❏ Strongly Agree
5.	Family members have up-to-date estate plans with wills, powers of attorney, and health care proxies. ❏ Strongly Disagree ❏ Disagree ❏ Possible ❏ Agree ❏ Strongly Agree
6.	Family members treat each other—and others in the business—with courtesy and respect. ❏ Strongly Disagree ❏ Disagree ❏ Possible ❏ Agree ❏ Strongly Agree
7.	Family members are capable. ❏ Strongly Disagree ❏ Disagree ❏ Possible ❏ Agree ❏ Strongly Agree
8.	Our policies and plans are based on our values, plans, and policies. ❏ Strongly Disagree ❏ Disagree ❏ Possible ❏ Agree ❏ Strongly Agree

9. Nonfamily members have been hired to fill positions family members are unable to fill well.

❏ Strongly Disagree ❏ Disagree ❏ Possible ❏ Agree ❏ Strongly Agree

10. Family members involved in the business know whether they are meeting expectations.

❏ Strongly Disagree ❏ Disagree ❏ Possible ❏ Agree ❏ Strongly Agree

11. We have a written succession plan that emphasizes qualifications and leadership skills.

❏ Strongly Disagree ❏ Disagree ❏ Possible ❏ Agree ❏ Strongly Agree

12. We have a compelling—and shared—vision of the future.

❏ Strongly Disagree ❏ Disagree ❏ Possible ❏ Agree ❏ Strongly Agree

13. Family members are trustworthy.

❏ Strongly Disagree ❏ Disagree ❏ Possible ❏ Agree ❏ Strongly Agree

14. Our decisions and actions are based on our values, plans, and policies.

❏ Strongly Disagree ❏ Disagree ❏ Possible ❏ Agree ❏ Strongly Agree

15. We have a board of directors that includes capable nonfamily members.

❏ Strongly Disagree ❏ Disagree ❏ Possible ❏ Agree ❏ Strongly Agree

16. Important decisions made at meetings are generally reflected in writing.

❏ Strongly Disagree ❏ Disagree ❏ Possible ❏ Agree ❏ Strongly Agree

17. We have a written business and strategic plan.

❏ Strongly Disagree ❏ Disagree ❏ Possible ❏ Agree ❏ Strongly Agree

18. We build from our successes and learn from our mistakes.

❏ Strongly Disagree ❏ Disagree ❏ Possible ❏ Agree ❏ Strongly Agree

19. Family members have strong interpersonal skills.

❏ Strongly Disagree ❏ Disagree ❏ Possible ❏ Agree ❏ Strongly Agree

20. There are consequences for violations of our values, plans, and policies.

❏ Strongly Disagree ❏ Disagree ❏ Possible ❏ Agree ❏ Strongly Agree

21. We have clear rules that govern who can work in our business—and how they advance.

❏ Strongly Disagree ❏ Disagree ❏ Possible ❏ Agree ❏ Strongly Agree

22. Decisions and actions are made and taken in a manner consistent with organizational structure.

❏ Strongly Disagree ❏ Disagree ❏ Possible ❏ Agree ❏ Strongly Agree

23. We have a fair compensation plan.

❏ Strongly Disagree ❏ Disagree ❏ Possible ❏ Agree ❏ Strongly Agree

24. Family members are encouraged to pursue their dreams and interests.

❏ Strongly Disagree ❏ Disagree ❏ Possible ❏ Agree ❏ Strongly Agree

25. Family members whose job performance is unacceptable incur appropriate consequences.

❏ Strongly Disagree ❏ Disagree ❏ Possible ❏ Agree ❏ Strongly Agree

26. We have a policy that addresses how "perks" are to be distributed.

❏ Strongly Disagree ❏ Disagree ❏ Possible ❏ Agree ❏ Strongly Agree

27. There is a good fit between the talent/interests of those who work in our business and the positions they hold.

❏ Strongly Disagree ❏ Disagree ❏ Possible ❏ Agree ❏ Strongly Agree

28. Family members are encouraged to constructively express their opinions.

❏ Strongly Disagree ❏ Disagree ❏ Possible ❏ Agree ❏ Strongly Agree

29. We have a buy-sell agreement that regulates transfer of ownership in our business.

❏ Strongly Disagree ❏ Disagree ❏ Possible ❏ Agree ❏ Strongly Agree

30. In the event of a disagreement, we strive for a constructive outcome.

❏ Strongly Disagree ❏ Disagree ❏ Possible ❏ Agree ❏ Strongly Agree

Notes

Preface

1. The term "stakeholder" is intended to capture the reality that one need not be a "shareholder" (or owner) to influence the management and decision making that takes place in a family business. Accordingly, the broader term "stakeholder" is intended to refer to owners, parents, nonactive sibling owners, spouses, and certain nonfamily members.

2. *See, e.g.*, George Stalk & Henry Foley, *Avoid the Traps That Can Destroy Family Businesses*, HARV. BUS. REV., Jan.–Feb. 2012, at 25, 25–26. *See also* WARD, J.L., KEEPING THE FAMILY BUSINESS HEALTHY (1987).

Chapter 1

1. George Stalk & Henry Foley, *Avoid the Traps That Can Destroy Family Businesses*, HARV. BUS. REV., Jan.–Feb. 2012, at 25.

2. KELIN E. GERSICK ET AL., GENERATION TO GENERATION: LIFE CYCLES OF THE FAMILY BUSINESS 25 (1997).

3. *Id.* at 2.

4. Family Business Alliance, Facts and Figures, http://www.fbagr.org/index .php?option=com_content&view=article&id=117&Itemid-75; *see also* B.M. BECKER & F.A. TILL-MAN, THE FAMILY-OWNED BUSINESS 22 (1978).

5. *See* Sabine B. Klein et al., *The F-PEC Scale of Family Influence: Construction, Validation, and Further Implication for Theory*, 29 ENTREPRENEURSHIP: THEORY & PRAC. 321 (2005).

6. *Samsung Boss Sued by Brother Over Father's Inheritance*, BBC NEWS (Jan. 28, 2013), http://www.bbc.co.uk/news/business-17025104.

7. *Exodus* 20:12.

8. *See* Elizabeth Dias, *Top Ten Family Feuds*, TIME, Aug. 23, 2011, http://www.time.com /time/specials/packages/article/0,28804,2089859_2089888_2089886,00.htm.

9. Nick Carbone, *Top 10 Family Feuds—Adidas vs. Puma*, TIME (Aug. 23, 2011), http:// www.time.com/time/specials/packages/article/0,28804,2089859_2089888_2089889,00.html.

10. *Id.*

11. Del Jones, *Pritzker Daughter Sues Family That Owns Hyatt Chain*, USA TODAY, Dec. 11, 2002, http://usatoday30.usatoday.com/money/industries/2002-12-11-pritzker_x.htm.

12. Jodi Wilgoren, *$900 Million Accord Enables Breakup of Pritzker Dynasty*, N.Y. TIMES, Jan. 7, 2005, https://www.nytimes.com/2005/01/07/national/07pritzkers.html.

13. *See, e.g.*, Leah McLaren, *Latner vs. Latner vs. Latner vs. Latner*, TORONTO LIFE, July 12, 2011, http://www.torontolife.com/daily/informer/from-print-edition-informer/2011/07/12/latner-vs-latner/.

14. *Id.* (emphasis added)

15. GARY MARCUS, KLUGE: THE HAPHAZARD EVOLUTION OF THE HUMAN MIND 45–46 (2009).

16. GRANT GORDON & NIGEL NICHOLSON, FAMILY WARS: CLASSIC CONFLICTS IN FAMILY BUSINESS AND HOW TO DEAL WITH THEM 12 (2010) (emphasis added).

17. STEPHEN M.R. COVEY, THE SPEED OF TRUST 1 (2008).

18. *See, e.g.*, LAURIE BETH JONES, JESUS, CEO: USING ANCIENT WISDOM FOR VISIONARY LEADERSHIP (1996); WHY BUSINESSMEN NEED PHILOSOPHY: THE CAPITALIST'S GUIDE TO THE IDEAS BEHIND AYN RAND'S *ATLAS SHRUGGED* (Debi Ghate & Richard E. Ralston eds., 2011).

19. A quick search on Google before this book went to press revealed only one article specifically on this opportunity to apply science to family business. That article happens to be one that I coauthored with my friend Dan Baker, a best-selling author on happiness and one of the first applied (as opposed to theoretical) positive psychologists.

Chapter 2

1. SHAWN ACHOR, THE HAPPINESS ADVANTAGE: THE SEVEN PRINCIPLES OF POSITIVE PSYCHOLOGY THAT FUEL SUCCESS AND PERFORMANCE AT WORK (2010).

2. *Id.* at 3 (emphasis added).

3. *Id.* at 21 (citing S. Lyubomirsky et al., *The Benefits of Frequent Positive Affect: Does Happiness Lead to Success?*, 131 PSYCHOL. BULL. 803 (2005)).

4. Stefan Lovgran, *Chimps, Humans 96 Percent the Same, Gene Study Finds*, NAT'L GEOGRAPHIC NEWS, August 31, 2005, www.news.nationalgeographic.com.

5. GARY MARCUS, KLUGE: THE HAPHAZARD EVOLUTION OF THE HUMAN MIND 2 (2009).

6. Sharon Begley, *In Our Messy, Reptilian Brains*, NEWSWEEK, Apr. 9, 2007, at 149.

7. DANIEL GARDNER, THE SCIENCE OF FEAR 23 (2008) (emphasis added).

8. GREGG JACOBS, THE ANCESTRAL MIND 29–30 (2003).

9. Atula, *Woman Saves Baby Girl from a Car Crashing into Their House*, GROWING YOUR BABY (Feb. 17, 2012), http://www.growingyourbaby.com/2012/02/17/woman-saves-baby-girl-from-a-car-crashing-into-their-house.

10. NASSIM TABEL, FOOLED BY RANDOMNESS: THE HIDDEN ROLE OF CHANCE IN LIFE AND IN THE MARKETS xlii (2d ed. 2008).

11. GARDNER, *supra* note 7, at 22–23.

12. JACOBS, *supra* note 8, at 55.

13. Brian Uzzi & Shannon Dunlap, *Managing Yourself: Make Your Enemies Your Allies*, HARV. BUS. REV., May 2012, at 134.

14. Michael M. Harris et al., *Keeping Up with the Joneses: A Field Study of the Relationships Among Upward, Lateral, and Downward Comparisons and Pay Level Satisfaction*, 93 J. APPLIED PSYCHOL. 665, 671 (2008) (emphasis added).

15. DAN BAKER, WHAT HAPPY PEOPLE KNOW 6–7 (2004).

16. ACHOR, *supra* note 1, at 41.

17. JACOBS, *supra* note 8, at 9–10.

18. BAKER, *supra* note 15, at 27–30.

19. *Id.*

20. DANIEL GOLEMAN, EMOTIONAL INTELLIGENCE 23 (1997).

21. Shelly L. Gable & Jonathan Haidt, *What (and Why) Is Positive Psychology?*, 9 REV. GEN. PSYCHOL. 103, 103 (2005).

22. MARTIN E.P. SELIGMAN, FLOURISH: A VISIONARY NEW UNDERSTANDING OF HAPPINESS AND WELL-BEING 10 (2011).

23. *See* Martin E. P. Seligman, *Positive Psychology, Positive Prevention, and Positive Therapy, in* HANDBOOK OF POSITIVE PSYCHOLOGY 3, 3–4 (C.R. Snyder & Shanc J. Lopez eds., 2002).

24. CHRISTOPHER PETERSON, A PRIMER IN POSITIVE PSYCHOLOGY 6 (2006).

25. P. Alex Linley & Stephen Joseph, *Applied Positive Psychology: A New Perspective for Professional Practice, in* POSITIVE PSYCHOLOGY IN PRACTICE 6 (P. Alex Linley & Stephen Joseph eds., 2004).

26. Bill George, *Mindfulness Helps You Become a Better Leader*, HARV. BUS. REV. BLOG NETWORK/HBS FACULTY (Oct. 26, 2012), https://blogs.hbr.org/hbsfaculty/2012/10/mindfulness -helps-you-become-a.html.

27. *Id.*

28. *How to Meditate: 10 Important Tips*, GOODLIFE ZEN (Jan. 28, 2013), http://goodlifezen .com/2008/04/18/how-to-start-meditating-ten-important-tips/.

29. Jill Hamburg Coplan, *How Positive Psychology Can Boost Your Business*, BUS. WK., Feb. 13, 2009, http://www.businessweek.com/magazine/content/09_62/s0902044518985.htm.

30. *See* MARTIN E.P. SELIGMAN, AUTHENTIC HAPPINESS: USING THE NEW POSITIVE PSYCHOLOGY TO REALIZE YOUR POTENTIAL FOR LASTING FULFILLMENT 66–69 (2002). *See also* MIHALY CSIKSZENTMIHALYI, FINDING FLOW: THE PSYCHOLOGY OF ENGAGEMENT WITH EVERYDAY LIFE 136 (1998) ("[T]he habit of rumination that our narcissistic society encourages actually might make things worse.").

31. PAUL PEARSALL, THE BEETHOVEN FACTOR: THE NEW POSITIVE PSYCHOLOGY OF HARDINESS, HAPPINESS, HEALING AND HOPE (2003).

32. Linley & Joseph, *supra* note 25, at 5–6.

33. ACHOR, *supra* note 1, at 22–23.

Chapter 3

1. GARY MARCUS, KLUGE 1 (2009).

2. E.J. Gitlay et al., *Dispositional Optimism and All-Cause and Cardiovascular Mortality in a Prospective Cohort of Elderly Dutch Men and Women*, 61 ARCHIVES GEN. PSYCHOL. 1126 (2004).

3. N. A. CHRISTAKIS & J. FOWLER, CONNECTED: THE SURPRISING POWER OF OUR SOCIAL NETWORKS AND HOW THEY SHAPE OUR LIVES (2009).

4. D. Keltner et al., *Fleeting Signs of the Course of Life: Facial Expression and Personal Adjustment*, 8 CURRENT DIRECTIONS PSYCHOL. SCI., 18 (1999).

5. D. GILBERT, STUMBLING ON HAPPINESS (2006); *see also* J. Schnitker, *Happiness and Success: Genes, Families, and the Psychological Effects of Socioeconomic Position and Social Support*, 114(S) AM. J. SOC. 233 (2008).

6. E.L. Gable et al., *What Do You Do When Things Go Right? The Intrapersonal and Inter-personal Benefits of Sharing Positive Events*, 87 J. PERSONALITY & SOC. PSYCHOL. 228 (2004).

7. M. Killingsworth, *The Future of Happiness Research*, HARV. BUS. REV., Jan.–Feb. 2012, at 88–89.

8. *Id.*

9. SHAWN ACHOR, THE HAPPINESS ADVANTAGE 41 (2010). *See also* S. Achor, *Positive Intelligence*, HARV. BUS. REV., Jan.–Feb. 2012, at 102.

10. SHAWN ACHOR, THE HAPPINESS ADVANTAGE: THE SEVEN PRINCIPLES OF POSITIVE PSYCHOLOGY THAT FUEL SUCCESS AND PERFORMANCE AT WORK 41–50 (2010).

11. Jill Hamburg Coplan, *How Positive Psychology Can Boost Your Business*, BUSINESS WEEK, Feb. 13, 2009, http://www.businessweek.com/stories/2009-02-12/how-positive-psychology -can-boost-your-business.

12. *See* ACHOR, *supra* note 10.

13. *See, e.g.*, Scott Friedman & Dan Baker, *Accentuate the Positive: The New Science of Positive Psychology Can Help Enterprising Families Achieve Sustainable Happiness and Business Success*, FAM. BUS. MAG., Summer 2010, at 64–66.

14. Barbara L. Frederickson, *The Value of Positive Emotions*, 91 AM. BEHAV. SCI. 330 (2003).

15. Barbara Frederickson et al., *The Undoing Effect of Positive Emotion*, 24(4) MOTIVATION & EMOTION 237, 238 (Dec. 2000) (emphasis added).

16. Barbara L. Frederickson & Marcial F. Losada, *Positive Affect and the Complex Dynamics of Human Flourishing*, 60 AM. PSYCHOL. 678 (2005). (The 3-to-1 positivity ratio is based on Marcial Losada's studies of group behavior at the Center for Advanced Research in Ann Arbor, Michigan, where he is the director. Losada, who was interested in measuring the effectiveness of teams, determined that teams with a positivity ratio of 2.9013 to 1 (simplified to 3-to-1) exhibited better working relationships than teams whose positive-to-negative interactions were below this ratio.)

17. BARBARA FREDRICKSON, POSITIVITY 277 (2009).

18. Frederickson & Losada, *supra* note 16, at 678–86.

19. *Id.* at 684.

20. Suzann Pileggi Pawelski, *The Happy Couple*, 21 SCI. AM. MIND, Summer 2012, at 50.

21. Coplan, *supra* note 11, at 2.

22. Gardiner Morse, *The Science Behind the Smile: An Interview with Professor Daniel Gilbert*, HARV. BUS. REV., Jan.–Feb. 2012, at 87.

23. Interview with David Cooperrider, HR.com (July 2001).

24. DAN BAKER, WHAT HAPPY PEOPLE KNOW 103 (2003).

25. THICH NHAT HANH, THE HEART OF THE BUDDHA'S TEACHING 41 (1999).

26. Rob May, *Reciprocal Altruism and Productivity*, Bus. Pundit (Apr. 12, 2004), http://www.businesspundit.com/reciprocal-altruism-and-productivity/ (emphasis added).

27. Larry Arnhart, *First Principles*, ISI Web J. (Aug. 1, 2011), http://www.firstprinciplesjournal.com/articles.aspx?article=690&theme=home&page=1&loc=b&type=cbtb (emphasis added).

28. Michael E. Porter & Mark R. Kramer, *Creating Shared Value*, Harv. Bus. Rev., January 2011, cited at http://hbr.org/2011/01/the-big-idea-creating-shared-value.

29. Stephen G. Post, *Altruism, Happiness, and Health: It's Good to Be Good*, 12 Int'l J. Behav. Med. 66 (2005) (emphasis added).

30. Flourishing: Positive Psychology and the Life Well-Lived xi, xviii (Corey Keyes & Jonathan Haidt eds., 2003).

31. J.P. Rushton, *The Altruistic Personality: Evidence from Laboratory, Naturalistic and Self-Report Perspectives*, in Development and Maintenance of Prosocial Behavior 271 (E. Staub et al. eds., 1984).

32. Christine Pearson & Christine Porath, The Cost of Bad Behavior: How Incivility Is Damaging Your Business and What to Do About It 4 (2009).

33. Spreitzer & C. Porath, *Creating Sustainable Performance*, Harv. Bus. Rev., Jan.–Feb. 2012, at 97.

34. Pearson & Porath, *supra* note 32, at 4 (2009) (citing W. Cascio & J. Boudreau, Investing in People: Financial Impact of Human Resources Initiatives (2008)).

35. Pearson & Porath, *supra* note 32, at 31.

36. Sue Shellenbarger, *Showing Appreciation at the Office? No, Thanks*, Wall St. J., Nov. 21, 2012, at D3.

37. Shawn Achor, *Positive Intelligence*, Harv. Bus. Rev., Jan.–Feb. 2012, at 102.

38. Josh Cable, *Studies Suggest Link Between Supportive Management Practices and Employee Wellness*, IndustryWeek, Nov. 19, 2009, http://www.industryweek.com/workforce/studies-suggest-link-between-supportive-management-practices-and-employee-wellness (suggesting a link between supportive management practices and employee wellness).

39. *Id.*

40. *See, e.g., Mark* 11:25 (Christianity); *Leviticus* 19:18 (Judaism and Christianity); *Qur'an,* 42:43 (Islam); *Dhammapada* 1-20 (Buddhism).

41. Alexander Pope, *An Essay on Criticism*, in Alexander Pope's Collected Poems 58, 71 (1924).

42. *See, e.g.,* Thomas M. Hubler, *Forgiveness as an Intervention in Family-Owned Business: A New Beginning*, 18 Fam. Bus. Rev. 95 (2005).

43. *See* Frederic Luskin, Forgive for Good 211–12 (2003).

44. Cary P. Cooper et al., Organizational Stress: A Review and Critique of Theory, Research and Applications (2001).

Chapter 4

1. Sue Shellenbarger, *When The Boss Is a Screamer*, Wall St. J., Aug. 15, 2012, at D1.

2. John Gordon, The Positive Dog: A Story About the Power of Positivity xiv (2012).

3. *Id.* at xiv–xv (citations omitted).

4. *Id.* at xii–xiii (citations omitted).

5. Shawn Achor, The Happiness Advantage: The Seven Principles of Positive Psychology That Fuel Success and Performance at Work 3—4 (2010) (emphasis added).

6. Jonathan Haidt, The Happiness Hypothesis: Finding Modern Truth in Ancient Wisdom 91 (2006) (citing Lyubomirsky et al., *Pursuing Happiness: The Architecture of Sustainable Change*, 2 Rev. Gen. Psychol. 111 (2005)).

7. Martin E.P. Seligman, Flourish: A Visionary New Understanding of Happiness and Well Being 9 (2011).

8. *Id.* at 10–11.

9. *Id.* at 16–20.

10. Mihaly Csikszentmihalyi, Flow: The Psychology of Optimal Experience 2 (1990).

11. *Id.* at 74.

12. *Id.* at 49.

13. *See* Gardiner Morse, *The Science Behind the Smile: An Interview with Professor Daniel Gilbert*, Harv. Bus. Rev., Jan.–Feb. 2012, at 88.

14. Steve Jobs, Stanford University 114th Commencement Address, June 12, 2005, http://www.forbes.com/sites/davidewalt/2011/10/10/steve-jobs-2005-stanford-commencement-address/.

15. Tom Rath, StrengthsFinder 2.0 11 (2007).

16. *Id.* at 12.

17. Marcus Buckingham & Donald O. Clifton, Now, Discover Your Strengths 5 (2001).

18. Daniel Kahneman, Thinking, Fast and Slow 13 (2011).

19. *Id.* at 12–13.

20. Csikszentmihalyi, Flow 152 (1990).

21. Ben Bernanke, Address to the International Association for Research in Income and Wealth, Aug. 8, 2012, http://www.policyshop.net/home/2012/8/8/fed-chief-looks-beyond-gdp-to-happiness-measures.html.

Chapter 5

1. *Matthew* 7:3–5.

2. Stephen Smith, *Heart Attack, Eh? Boss May Be Cause*, Boston Globe, Nov. 25, 2008 (cited in Christine Pearson & Christine Porath, The Cost of Bad Behavior: How Incivility Is Damaging Your Business and What to Do About It x (2009)).

3. Dale Carnegie, How to Win Friends and Influence People 13 (Simon & Schuster 1981).

4. Sanjiv Chopra & David Fisher, Leadership by Example: The Ten Key Principles of All Great Leaders 22 (2012).

5. Christopher Chabris & Daniel Simons, The Invisible Gorilla: How Our Intuitions Deceive Us 85 (2011).

6. *Id.* at 122.

7. *Id.* at 154.

8. *Id.* at 186.

9. *Id.* at 22 (citing Donald A. Redelmeier & Robert J. Tibshirani, *Association Between Cellular-Telephone Calls and Motor Vehicle Collisions*, 336 NEW ENG. J. MED. 453, 453–58 (1997)).

10. DEBORAH TANNEN, YOU JUST DON'T UNDERSTAND: WOMEN AND MEN IN CONVERSATION 17 (2001).

11. Sherry Turkle, *The Flight from Conversation*, N.Y. TIMES, April 21, 2012, http://www.nytimes.com/2012/04/22/opinion/sunday/the-flight-from-conversation.html?pagewanted=all&_r=0.

12. Albert Mehrabian & Susan Ferris, *Inference of Attitudes from Nonverbal Communication in Two Channels*, 31(3) J. CONSULTING PSYCHOL. 248, 252 (1967).

13. Alex Pentland, *To Signal Is Human*, 98 AM. SCI. 203, 204 (2010).

14. *See id.*

15. LEO TOLSTOY, ANNA KARENINA 347 (Penguin Classics 2000).

16. DANIEL L. SCHACTER, THE SEVEN SINS OF MEMORY: HOW THE MIND FORGETS AND REMEMBERS 16 (2002).

17. *Id.* at 45.

18. *Id.* at 94.

19. *Id.* at 113.

20. *Id.*

21. *Id.* at 33.

22. *See* DANIEL L. SCHACTER, THE SEVEN SINS OF MEMORY 13–14 (2001) (discussing early experiments by Hermann Ebbinghaus).

23. GARY MARCUS, KLUGE: THE HAPHAZARD EVOLUTION OF THE HUMAN MIND 36–37 (2009).

24. DANIEL ARIELY, THE (HONEST) TRUTH ABOUT DISHONESTY: HOW WE LIE TO EVERYONE—ESPECIALLY OURSELVES 23 (2012).

25. *Id.* at 27.

26. *Id.* at 27.

27. *Id.* at 201, 206–7.

28. Quoted in Robert Lee Hotz, *Science Reveals Why We Brag So Much*, WALL ST. J., May 7, 2012 (citing studies by Diana Tamir and Jason Mitchell), http://online.wsj.com/article/sb10001429052702304451104577390392329291890.html.

29. PHILLIP HUNSAKER AND TONY ALESSANDRA, THE NEW ART OF MANAGING PEOPLE 164 (2008).

30. John Baldoni, *Humility as a Leadership Trait*, HARV. BUS. REV., Sept. 15, 2009, http://blogs.hbr.org/baldoni/2009/09/humility_as_a_leadership_trait.html.

31. *Id.*

32. Bradley P. Owens, Michael D. Johnson & Terrence R. Mitchell, *Humility in Organizations: Implications for Performance, Teams and Leadership* 24, 25 ORG. SCI., http://dx.doi.org/101287/orsc.1120.0795.

33. *Humility Key to Effective Leadership*, SCI. DAILY (Dec. 9, 2011), http://www.sciencedaily.com/releases/2011/12/111208173643.htm (citing work by Professor Owens and Professor David Hekman).

34. Quoted in Sean Eichenberger, *The Best Family Businesses*, Forbes.com (June 17, 2011), http://www.forbes.com/2011/06/17/best-family-businesses.html.

35. *See* James Olan Hutcheson, *The End of a 1,400-Year-Old Business*, Bloomberg Bus. Wk. (Apr. 16, 2007), http://www.businessweek.com/stories/2007-04-16/the-end-of-a-1-400-year-old -businessbusinessweek-business-news-stock-market-and-financial-advice.

Chapter 6

1. Robert Howard, *Values Make the Company: An Interview with Robert Haas*, Harv. Bus. Rev., Mar. 3, 1990, at 35.

2. Frank J. Sulloway, Born to Rebel: Birth Order, Family Dynamics, and Creative Lives xiii, xv (1997) (emphasis added).

3. James E. Hughes Jr., Family Wealth—Keeping It in the Family: How Family Members and Their Advisers Preserve Human, Intellectual, and Financial Assets for Generations 21 (2004).

4. Grant Gordon & Nigel Nichelson, Family Wars: Classic Conflicts in Family Business and How to Deal with Them 36–37 (2008).

5. *See, e.g.*, Andy Gardner & Per T. Smiseth, *Evolution of Parental Care Driven by Mutual Reinforcement of Parental Food Provisioning and Sibling Competition*, Proc. Royal Soc'y B (July 28, 2010), http://www.zoo.ox.ac.uk/group/gardner/publications/GardnerSmiseth_2011.pdf.

6. Gordon & Nichelson, *supra* note 4, at 164.

7. Hughes Jr., *supra* note 3, at 22.

8. Lilach Sagiv, Sonia Roccas & Osnat Hazan, *Value Pathways to Well-Being: Healthy Values Valued Goal Attainment, and Environmental Congruence*, reprinted in Positive Psychology in Practice 75 (Linley and Joseph eds.) (2004).

9. Jeffrey Abrahams, The Mission Statement Book: 301 Corporate Mission Statements from America's Top Companies 16 (2004).

10. Jim Collins & Jerry I. Porras, Built to Last: Successful Habits of Visionary Companies 55 (2002) (emphasis removed).

11. Christopher Peterson, A Primer in Positive Psychology 167 (2006).

12. *Id.* at 169.

13. *See, e.g.*, Aaron Jarden, Presentation at the New Zealand Psychological Society (2008), https://docs.google.com/viewer?a=v&q=cache:fX5wv7JDwlMJ:www.aaronjarden.com/uploads/3/8/0/4/3804146/2008_-_individual_well-being_and_its_relationship_to_personal_values_psychopathology_and_character_strengths.ppt+Aaron+Jarden,+Individual+Well-being+and+its'+Relationship+to+Personal+values,+Psychopathology,+and+Character+Strengths,+Presentation+at+The+New+Zealand+Psychological+Society&hl=en&gl=us&pid=bl&srcid=ADGEESjvWCTdQIoyJ5LnilSjt2atfgcLh_RYFtCSedj2Nrf2XJ1Bl-evbUrKdqFmKblq2IWpxBSzTGE49s_yDu-Fh7O3OaGsBqRs8L0jlzltcaE6xA8QJqMwGTRmPBSM0BTCi4aHeyc2&sig=AHIEtbQHipPKZQrV89DGkC5O_Uk1ZxZUZQ).

14. Christopher Peterson & Martin Seligman, Character Strengths and Virtues: A Handbook and Classification 625–33 (2004).

15. *Id.*

16. Robert Spector & Patrick D. McCarthy, The Nordstrom Way to Customer Service Excellence: The Handbook for Becoming the "Nordstrom" of Your Industry 19 (1996).

17. *Id.* at 124.

18. Gretchen Spreitzer & Christine Porath, *Creating Sustainable Performance*, Harv. Bus. Rev., Jan. 2012, at 94.

19. Sanjiv Chopra & David Fisher, Leadership by Example: The Ten Key Principles of All Great Leaders 55 (2012).

20. James C. Collins & Jerry I. Porras, *Building Your Company's Vision*, Harv. Bus. Rev., Sept.–Oct. 1996, at 72. *See also* Jim Collins & Jerry I. Porras, Built to Last: Successful Habits of Visionary Companies 233 (2002).

21. Lilach Sagiv & Shalom H. Schwartz, *Cultural Values in Organizations: Insights from Europe*, 1 Eur. J. Int'l Mgmt. 176, 183 (2007) (citations omitted).

22. Justin Doebele, *The Softest Pillow*, Forbes (Sept. 2, 2002), http://www.forbes.com/global/2002/0902/036.html.

23. Linda C. McClain, *Family Constitutions and the (New) Constitution of the Family*, 75 Fordham L. Rev., 833, 835 (2006).

Chapter 7

1. Kat McGowan, *Introduction*, Discover Magazine's Special Report on the Brain, Fall 2012, at 5.

2. Daniel Kahneman, Thinking, Fast and Slow 4 (2011).

3. *Board of Directors*, Walmart, http://corporate.walmart.com/our-story/leadership/board-of-directors.

4. Shelley Farrington et al., *The Influence of Family and Non-family Stakeholders on Family Business Success*, 3 South African J. Entrepreneurship & Small Bus. Mgmt. 32, 41 (2010) (citations omitted) (emphasis supplied).

5. John Davis, *Organizing the Family-Run Business*, Harv. Bus. School Working Knowledge (Oct. 1, 2001), http://hbswk.hbs.edu/item/2536.html.

6. Janis, I.L., *Groupthink*, 5 (6) Psychol. Today 43–46, 74–76 (Nov. 1971).

7. *See* David Brooks, *The Machiavellian Temptation*, N.Y. Times, Mar. 1, 2012, http://www.nytimes.com/2012/03/02/opinion/brooks-the-machiavellian-temptation.html.

8. Dan Ariely, Predictably Irrational xviii–xix (2010).

9. *See* Dean R. Fowler, Ph.D., Spouses and The Family Council, Dean Fowler Associates, Inc. 200 S. Executive Drive #101 Brookfield, WI 53005, http://www.deanfowler.com/wp-content/themes/metric/articles/spouses_and_the_family_council.pdf.

Chapter 8

1. Philip Zimbardo, The Lucifer Effect: Understanding How Good People Turn Evil 266 (2007).

2. Challenger Disaster—A NASA Tragedy, http://space.about.com/cs/challenger/a/challenger.htm.

3. Ira Bryck, *Get Off The Same Page!*, UMass Amherst Family Business Center, http://www.umass.edu/fambiz/articles/directors_desk/get_off_page.html.

4. James Larsen, Ph.D., *Business Practice Findings*, Bus. Psychol., http://businesspsych.org/articles/135.html (referencing Menon et al., *The Quality and Effectiveness of Marketing Strategy: Effects of Functional and Dysfunctional Conflict in Intraorganizational Relationships*, 24 J. Acad. Mktg. Sci. 299 (1996)).

5. *Id.*

6. Jeff Thompson, *Have a Conflict? Use FAVES*, Psychology Today (Apr. 10, 2012), http://www.psychologytoday.com/blog/beyond-words/201204/have-conflict-use-faves.

7. American Psychological Association—Anger, http://www.apa.org/topics/anger/index.aspx.

8. Leslie Wayne, *Brother Versus Brother; Koch Family's Long Legal Feud Is Headed for a Jury*, N.Y. Times, Apr. 28, 1998, http://www.nytimes.com/1998/04/28/business/brother-versus-brother-koch-family-s-long-legal-feud-is-headed-for-a-jury.html.

9. Andrew Newberg & Mark Robert Waldman, Words Can Change Your Brain: 12 Conversation Strategies That Build Trust, Resolve Conflict, and Increase Intimacy 3–4 (2012).

10. *Id.*

11. Frans B.M. de Waal, *Primates—A Natural Heritage of Conflict Resolution*, 289 Sci. 586, 589 (July 28, 2000).

12. *Id.* at 590.

13. Ken Binmore, Game Theory: A Very Short Introduction 1 (2007).

14. *See* Robert Axelrod, The Evolution of Cooperation (revised ed., 2006). Robert Axelrod on Six Advances in Cooperation Theory (July 2000), http://www.personal.umich.edu/~axe/research/sixadvances.pdf.

15. *See* Deborah L. Cohen, *Not Playing Games: Firm Takes Decision-Making Theory into Transactions*, ABA J. (Jan. 2013), http://www.abajournal.com/mobile/mag_article/not_playing_games_firm_takes_decision-making_theory_into_transactions.

16. Linda K. Wray & Deborah Clemmensen, *Collaborative Practice: Lawyer as Negotiator and Problem-Solver*, http://www.ramseybar.org/PDFs/collaborative_practice_long.pdf.

Chapter 9

1. Diana Loomans, *If I Had My Child to Raise Over Again*, 100 Ways to Build Self-Esteem & Teach Values (2004), http://www.dianaloomans.com/child.htm.

2. Brian Sullivan, *Pass the Subpoena, Please: Intrafamily Squabbling Could Put a Damper on Holiday Feast Gobbling*, ABA J. (Oct. 13, 2012), http://www.abajournal.com/magazine/article/pass_the_subpoena_please_intrafamily_squabbling_could_put_a_damper_on_holid/.

3. Don Bradley & Lance Burroughs, *A Strategy for Family Business Succession Planning*, http://sbaer.uca.edu/research/SBI/2010/p05.pdf.

4. Positive Psychology in Practice 561–78 (P. Alex Linley & Stephen Joseph eds., 2012).

5. 10 Tips for Happy Retirement Living—Make the Most of the Rest of Your Life, http://seniorliving.about.com/od/retirement/a/retirement_livi.htm.

6. Mark Glover, *A Therapeutic Jurisprudential Framework of Estate Planning*, 37 Seattle U. L. Rev. 427, 429 (2012) (citations omitted).

7. *Id.*

8. Gordon Pitts, In the Blood: Battles to Succeed in Canada's Family Businesses, quoted at Ron Foreman, *Family Business Stories & Quotations*, June 24, 2003, http://ronforeman.com/2003/06/24/family-business-stories-quotations/.

9. Sheldon Adelson Quotes & Sayings, http://www.searchquotes.com/quotes/author/Sheldon_Adelson/.

10. Ivan Landsberg, Succeeding Generations 340 (1999).

11. *Id.*

12. *Id.*

13. *See* Rashmi Kumar, *Richemont Family Chief to Step Down—Names Two Non-Family Successors*, Campden FB (Nov. 9, 2012), http://www.campdenfb.com/article/richemont-family-chief-step-down-names-two-non-family-successors.

Chapter 10

1. Scott Friedman & Bob Rich, Secrets from the Delphi Café: Unlocking the Code to Happiness 157 (2006).

2. Kevin Davis, *Brain Trials: Neuroscience Is Taking a Stand in the Courtroom*, ABA J. (Nov. 1, 2012), http://www.abajournal.com/magazine/article/brain_trials_neuroscience_is_taking_a_stand_in_the_courtroom/.

Index

A

ABA Journal, 145, 156
Abrahams, Jeffrey, 97
Absentmindedness, 80
Accountability, 102, 115
Achor, Shawn, 14, 24, 32, 38, 39, 61
Acknowledgement, 85
Active listener, 84
Adelson, Sheldon Gary, 163
Adidas, 4, 77
Affluenza, 154
AI. *See* Appreciative Inquiry (AI)
Alessandra, Anthony J., 83–84
Altruism, 46–48
Altruism, Happiness, and Health
    (Post), 48
Amazon.com vision statement, 105
American Airlines, 72
American Psychological Association,
    37, 138
Ancestral brain. *See also* Brain
    diminished trust and, 19
    fight-or-flight response, 15–17, 19
    perception of threats and, 17–18
The Ancestral Mind (Jacobs), 16
Angelou, Maya, 11
Anger, 24
Anger management, 138–140
Anna Karenina (Tolstoy), 38, 79
Appreciation, 43–46, 49

Appreciative Inquiry (AI), 43–44
Ariely, Dan, 82, 119
Arnhart, Larry, 47
Arrogance, 23
Assessments, 65–66
Astrachan, Joseph, 2
Audit committee, 122
Augustine of Hippo, 90
Authentic Happiness (Seligman), 29
Authentic Leadership (George), 30
Authority, 85, 117–118
Axelrod, Robert M., 143

B

Back to Methuselah (Shaw), 104
Baker, Dan, 22, 26–27, 45
Baldoni, John, 84–85
Bar-On EQ, 66
Baylor College of Medicine, 169
Bay of Pigs invasion, 135
BBC News, 3
Begley, Sharon, 15
Benefits plans, 155–156
Bernanke, Ben, 68
Bias, 80
Bible, 3
Binmore, Ken, 142
Blink (Gladwell), 111
Blocking, 80
Bloomberg Businessweek, 31

About the Author

Scott Friedman, the author of five books and numerous articles on family business dynamics and planning strategies, works closely with family businesses and their advisors across the United States. A frequent lecturer on the subject, Friedman is also the creator of The Family Business Scorecard, a proprietary assessment tool he uses in working with family businesses. Friedman is the managing partner of Lippes Mathias Wexler Friedman LLP, a law firm in Buffalo, New York, and the manager of Next Gen Advisors, LLC, a family business advisory company that works with family businesses and their professional advisors. He also works closely with the University at Buffalo's School of Management and Center for Entrepreneurial Leadership in developing educational and practical programs for family businesses.